THE GOSPEL ACCORDING TO VIDEO GAMES

JARED DEES

_____

For more information, visit jareddees.com.

Paperback: ISBN 978-1-954135-12-3
eBook: ISBN 978-1-954135-13-0

For Carlo

Thank you for the prayers.

CONTENTS

PART THREE
THE CHURCH

PART FOUR
THE ENEMIES

PART FIVE
GAMEPLAY GUIDE

PART SIX
BEATING THE GAME

AUTHOR'S NOTE

Can anything beat the feeling of booting up a new video game for the first time? The opening screen appears, and we are welcomed into a whole new world. Adventure awaits. Hours of excitement, struggle, failure, success, and victory are ahead. At the same time, the game of life is well underway. But this game is real. We will struggle, fail, succeed, and enjoy what God has ready to share with us in life. Thankfully, we won't have to play alone.

Welcome. This book is an opportunity to geek out about God and video games. We will combine these two loves in order to deepen our understanding of the role God plays in our lives. Each short chapter will express the gospel message of Jesus Christ using metaphors from some of the best video games of all time.

Video games have not been around for long compared to the long history of Christianity. Yet video games have become a significant part of many people's lives today. Some people may understand video games much better than Christianity. (I know I did when I first embraced my faith in Jesus Christ.) Therefore, the connections between the games and the message of good news are meant to offer new ways of seeing the basics of the Christian message.

The metaphors are symbolic and often abstract. There is no expectation that the game designers and developers intended any of the theological propositions put forth here. Very few, if any, of the connections you read here were ever in the minds of the incredible people who created the games. The connections are a fun way to remember great games by linking them to the Christian life.

With every metaphor comes a limitation. When you read about a connection here, understand that there will always be more to say about a topic. This book is no theological treatise. If anything, it is an invitation to learn more. The message of good news is always an introduction, but as a person becomes a disciple, the hunger to learn more leads them to study more deeply and directly.

You will find no judgments about the morality of each of the games presented here. This book is not meant to align Christianity with or against any video game, genre, developer, or system. I hope to avoid any debates about the morality of the games no matter how graphic or offensive they might be to someone new to them. Instead, I try to start each chapter with a game familiar to the reader and take them toward a better understanding of the truths within the gospel. I do not apply the gospel message to the choice of playing a particular game.

By using metaphors to explain the gospel, I also run the risk of stating inaccuracies about Christianity. As Christians, we call these inaccuracies heresies. I take full blame for any mistake you will read here and ask for mercy in my attempt to take readers on a journey of faith. My goal is less about defining doctrine and more about igniting joy in the hearts of those who love video games to see Christianity in a new way. In other words, I hope to transfer the joy of gaming into the joy of God.

One final note for seasoned Christians. As this is a presentation of the gospel, not Christian dogma, I make no attempt to sway readers toward one denomination or another. To do so would be like convincing someone with a Nintendo in the 1990s that Sega Genesis was better, or vice versa. Instead, I will restate the words C. S. Lewis shared in the preface of *Mere Christianity*: "There is no mystery about my own position. . . . But in this book I am not trying to convert anyone to my own position."[1]

In fact, conversion is not on my mind at all at least in the sense of identifying oneself in a particular way. I do hope, however, that readers will share with me a love of video games along with a newfound or re-found love of God. If you have ever found joy in gaming, I know that you will be able to find joy in God.

Jared Dees

PART ONE
GETTING STARTED

CHAPTER 1
IT'S DANGEROUS TO GO ALONE! TAKE THIS

In the original version of Nintendo's *The Legend of Zelda*, a player begins the game with no weapons. On the starting screen, however, there is an easily discovered cave. Inside that cave is an old man who says the now classic line, "It's dangerous to go alone! Take this."

Standing below him is a sword. It is the first of many tools that Link, the game's hero, will use to save Princess Zelda. There are so many connections to real life in this short exchange.

First, the old man points out the deepest, universal fear in all of us. We are afraid to be alone. This same fear is intermingled with a fear of death. It is this fear of death and rejection that motivates the way we interact with one another. We all want to be accepted and loved.

Second, Christianity has good news to offer. In fact, the word "gospel" comes from the Greek word meaning "good news." The four gospels in the Bible share the good news about Jesus Christ's life and teachings. The Gospel of Mark even opens with the words announcing "the beginning of the good news of Jesus Christ" (Mark 1:1). That good news, put simply, is that we are not alone. God loves us so much that he became one of us, died for us, and rose so that we might rise with him as well.

The gospel is like the sword in *The Legend of Zelda*. We don't have to go alone through life. We are like the many outcasts that Jesus forgave and healed in the Bible. They no longer had reason to feel alone. Armed with the good news, we know that God is with us and we don't have to be afraid.

CHAPTER 2
INSTRUCTION MANUAL FOR LIFE

Before digital downloads, home console video games came with instruction booklets packaged in the original boxes. These instruction manuals began with diagrams describing how to use the controller and navigate the game. They also included a backstory for the game and tips or tutorials on how to play the beginning levels.

Christianity comes with a book as well: the Bible. In some ways the Bible is like an instruction manual. It includes backstory about God and his people. There are many different instructions for living, like the Ten Commandments, the Beatitudes, Jesus's Sermon on the Mount, Saint Paul's letters and advice, etc. Referencing the Bible will help Christians find ways to live a better life. The Word of God is "a lamp to my feet and a light to my path" (Psalm 119:105).

But a video game instruction booklet is unlike the Bible in one essential way. The Bible is the inspired Word of God. It is more than just a collection of stories and teachings for us to learn how to live life. Through these sacred Scriptures, God speaks directly to his people. We can encounter Jesus

Christ in a prayerful reading of the Word of God today and every day for the rest of our lives.

Unlike an instruction manual, which is often helpful and sometimes interesting, the Bible can be helpful, interesting, but most of all transformative. "The word of God is living and active and sharper than any two-edged sword, piercing until it divides soul from spirit, joints from marrow; it is able to judge the thoughts and intentions of the heart" (Hebrews 4:12). God can transform our hearts and minds while we read his Word.

You will read references to Scripture throughout this book with citations in parentheses pointing you to each book, chapter, and verse. These citations are more than wise words. These words are opportunities to reflect and open up to God speaking directly to us.

CHAPTER 3
PRESS START

Almost every video game begins with the same screen. To play you must press the Start button.

It may seem simple, but there is an important metaphor in the simple act of pressing Start.

To watch a movie, you press the Play button. The movie plays, and we become passive observers. It goes on without any other action on our part. It begins and ends as we watch and enjoy.

A video game, on the other hand, requires our active participation. We are in control of what happens during the game. The game requires us to make choices and experience the consequences.

Our lives are more like video games than movies. We are active agents in the world. In Christianity we call this "free will." God gives us the gift to choose and a conscience to help us make the right choices.

God does not act like the director of a movie, choosing for us to perform in a certain way. He creates the world like a video game designer and helps us progress through the adventure as we make our own choices along the way. No single path to get to the end of the game is exactly the same, but the destination is always there waiting for us.

Press Start on life. Take responsibility for your actions and get into the game. There is so much to enjoy along the way. God has such a great adventure planned for you.

CHAPTER 4
MINECRAFT CREATION STORY

Click on the Create New World button in *Minecraft* and an entire universe is created in seconds. Suddenly you appear in a blocky, unexplored world with endless possibilities. *Minecraft* is called a sandbox game, meaning players have the freedom to use creativity to make their own goals and to build or explore the world.

It is hard not to make a connection between the Bible's creation story and *Minecraft*. According to the story in Genesis, God created the world in seven days. Each day signified a new part of God's creation: light, sky, ground, plants, celestial objects, animals, etc. At the end of each day, God saw that what he had made was good.

We get to experience the wonder and goodness of God's creation every day. We see the light and darkness, the water and the land, the animals of the sky and dry land. We get to look with appreciation on the good in our world just like a freshly created universe in *Minecraft* with light and darkness, green and brown ground, plants, stars, sun, moon, and many living things that swim in the sea or creep upon the ground.

On the sixth day God finally created human beings and, like *Minecraft*, gave the new world to them to explore. He even gave them dominion over "every creeping thing that creeps upon the earth" (Genesis 1:26) just as *Minecraft* players have dominion over the creepers and other living mobs (mobile objects) in the game.

We were created unlike anything else in the Creation story. It says in Genesis that humans were made in God's image and likeness (Genesis 1:27). In that likeness of God, we are creators like him. We were given the ability to expand, explore, and craft new creations. As a *Minecraft* character creates with endless possibilities, so too do we enjoy the freedom of creativity in the world today. Made in God's image and likeness, we get to craft and create goodness in the world just like the one who created us.

CHAPTER 5
TWO-PLAYER GAME

In 1972 the first commercially successful video game debuted. It was a simple concept, and people loved it.

Pong was based on the game of table tennis (also known as Ping-Pong). In the *Pong* video game, two small lines shift up and down the screen to bounce the tiny white dot of the ball back and forth. Just like table tennis, you score points by getting the ball past the other "paddle."

There are many kinds of video games: one-player games, two-player games, and multiplayer games. Let's not forget, however, that the first successful video game was meant to be a two-player game. Whether playing another person or against the computer, the concept of "beating the game" as a single player came later.

Life is also a two-player game. We are not alone. We are not meant to be alone. God is with us. People are here with us too. We play with companions. Sometimes we compete against each other, and sometimes we support one another in both video games and in life. Your life was never meant to be a single-player game.

In the story of the Garden of Eden, Eve was created as a partner for Adam. "It is not good that the man should be alone," God said (Genesis 2:18). Remember, in life you don't have to go alone. People are there for you. God is there for you. Always select two-player mode on the game of life if you can. You never have to play alone.

CHAPTER 6
TAKE OR DROP

The early computer role-playing games (RPGs) of the 1970s and '80s were simple text-based adventures. Games like *Zork* (1977) and *Adventureland* (1978) were inspired by the tabletop game *Dungeons & Dragons* and J. R. R. Tolkien's classic series *The Lord of the Rings*. Like a Dungeon Master in *D&D*, players in early RPGs read a text-based description of a scene and then responded with simple commands like *take knife*, *drop knife*, *open*, *close*, *ask*, *go*, *look*, etc.

The ability to make choices was a breakthrough in early video game design. These RPGs were programmed to respond to certain commands and adapt the story to the choices of the players. This ability to choose transformed gaming just like it transformed the human race in real life.

The idea of free will is essential to understand humanity and Christianity. As human beings we have the ability to choose, and there are consequences for those choices. There are negative effects for doing evil and positive effects for good choices.

The story of the fall of Adam and Eve in Genesis expresses the impact of free will. Imagine if the story was written like a text-based RPG. The players, Adam and Eve, might read something like this:

"You stand in the Garden of Eden near the Tree of Knowledge. A SERPENT appears next to the tree."

Eve: TALK TO SERPENT

"The Serpent says, 'You will not die if you eat from this tree, for God knows that when you eat of it your eyes will be opened, and you will be like God, knowing good and evil.'"

Eve: EAT FRUIT

Adam is standing nearby. Would you like to offer him some of the fruit?

Eve: GIVE FRUIT TO ADAM

Then, of course, Adam has a choice. What does he choose?

Not "DROP FRUIT" but "TAKE FRUIT" and "EAT FRUIT."

GAME OVER.

Adam and Eve will be banished from the garden and die.

You have free will too. You have the ability to make choices in response to what you see and hear in the world. Those choices have consequences, and the story of your life continues, like an RPG reacting to those choices. To win the game, you must complete the adventure. To complete the adventure, you must make good choices along the way. Thankfully, we are not alone. God sent his only Son to die so that we can recover from poor choices and live.

CHAPTER 7
A FALL LIKE FORTNITE

Fortnite is one of the most popular games of the early twenty-first century and became a cultural phenomenon. The game also provides an interesting metaphor about the spiritual life.

Fortnite: Battle Royale is a player-versus-player game of survival. Players begin the game on a "Battle Bus" flying over the game map, then they fall from the bus toward the battle. Once they land, they scavenge for weapons, defend themselves, and defeat others to become the last fighter standing.

As a human race we experienced a fall as well. Genesis 2–3 tells the story of the fall of Adam and Eve. God created Adam and Eve and placed them in the peaceful Garden of Eden. He told them not to eat from the Tree of Knowledge of Good and Evil. The cunning Serpent tempted Eve to eat from the Tree and she gave the fruit to Adam to eat as well. As a punishment for this first sin (Original Sin), Adam and Eve were banished from Eden. This is what Christians refer to as the "Fall."

What are people like after the Fall? In the next story, Cain kills his brother Abel. Because of pride, jealousy, anger, and many more vices, humans compete and even kill one another. The survival instinct is powerful and leads to destruction.

We are much like the falling *Fortnite* characters who fight to survive. Fighting for survival is not God's original plan. He offered us peace and unity with him, and we lost it through sin leading us into a world of division and violence against one another.

Thankfully, our story did not end there. Jesus Christ is the new Adam. He willingly gave up his life and died so that he could restore peace and unity with God and one another. "For as all die in Adam, so all will be made alive in Christ" (1 Corinthians 15:22). Through Christ we have new life and do not need to compete to survive.

In fact, Christ taught us to turn the other cheek. He taught us to love God and love our neighbors as ourselves. He taught us to love others as he loved us, giving up his life for us. It would be like playing a game of *Fortnite* but only working to help others survive—even giving up our lives so that others may live. Because in Jesus Christ we have life everlasting. Death no longer has hold on us. He is the last Adam and gave us his life-giving spirit (1 Corinthians 15:45).

CHAPTER 8
THE CALIBER OF A SOUL

What is our soul? If you follow the reasoning behind the popular weapon-fighting video game *Soulcalibur*, the soul is what gives something life. In that series a sword becomes sentient after being infused with a soul, and this bad weapon takes on the name "Soul Edge." In the second installment of the series, the "Soul Calibur" is introduced in opposition to the evil Soul Edge. The name is derived from King Arthur's famous Excalibur sword. All of this lore exists as background plot to what most see as an enjoyable series of fighting games.

Our bodies were infused with souls to give us life as well. "The LORD God formed man from the dust of the ground and breathed into his nostrils the breath of life, and the man became a living being" (Genesis 2:7). A human being is both body and soul united as one human person, and it is the soul that we often use to describe what sets us apart from animals, as man was made in God's image and likeness. While the body may die, it is the soul that lives on after death.

The soul is a gift directly from God. While our bodies are formed from our human parents, it is God who gives us a soul. Along with this soul comes a destiny to be forever united with him in heaven or separated from God in hell. It is in the inner depths of our being that we may choose to turn toward or away from God.

According to Jesus, the greatest commandment is in Deuteronomy 6:5: "You shall love the Lord your God with all your heart and with all your soul and with all your mind" (Matthew 22:37). The more we love God, the more our souls are united with him and will remain united with him even after our death.

The word *caliber* means "quality of character" or the "level of ability." It is unrelated to the root of the word Excalibur or *Soulcalibur*. There are no evil souls like the Soul Edge. Within the soul we find our hearts and our free will to choose to love God. This choice is what gives us a high quality of character. This is what makes us human. This is what we will discover as our true purpose in life.

CHAPTER 9
SIN LIKE SNOOD

During the early 2000s, it seemed like everyone was playing a computer game called *Snood*. *Snood* was a puzzle game with a cannon at the bottom of the screen that shot "snoods" (little monster icons). When a snood attached to two other snoods of the same kind, they disappeared. Once you cleared all of the snoods, you beat the level.

The game was great, but there were two problems with the version of *Snood* people were downloading onto computers in the early days of the Internet. First, the game itself was highly addicting. Teenagers and college students were playing the game and procrastinating on schoolwork instead of studying for their calculus exams.

The second problem was that the pirated free version being downloaded from the Internet almost always contained a computer virus. This was not the fault of the video game creators. The viruses were added on later by hackers and spread to ignorant kids and college students. Inevitably computers glitched or lost speed when down-loading the program.

Everyone knew the game was addicting. Everyone knew the game came with possible computer viruses. We downloaded and played it anyway.

It's hard not to make a connection to the Christian idea of sin. Sins are too often thought of as bad things we do. More than simply bad choices, our sins are addicting habits. They are hard to resist, and the more we sin, the harder it is to resist the sin. Sin is a lot like playing just one more round of your favorite video game. It's hard to say no.

The bad part about sin, however, is more than just the pain we cause ourselves. Sin acts like a computer virus. The sin invades our lives and affects everything else we try to do. The sooner that sin can be wiped away, the better our lives will become.

CHAPTER 10
THE SIMS AND SINS

When *The Sims* released in February 2000, the concept might have sounded lame to gamers. Players create and control simulated people living everyday, ordinary lives? They eat meals, watch TV, read, go to work, buy a home, and maintain relationships with other simulated people? Sounds boring, right?

The Sims was a breakout success and sold more than eleven million copies to become the best-selling PC game of its time. A series of expansion packs and sequel games followed in the years to come.

There is no set story line in *The Sims*. There are no bosses or bad guys. There is technically no way to win the game. There are no essential goals for players to accomplish other than survival. Yet people love creating and becoming their simulated people.

Life can feel a lot like a simulation. There isn't necessarily a bad guy to overcome. We don't have monsters attacking us. We spend our days eating, working, seeking entertainment, and growing in our relationships.

Christianity provides purpose to playing the game of life. From the Christian perspective, there is an enemy and monsters to defeat. There is a game to be played beyond simply external survival. The game is played within our heads and our hearts.

Put simply, the enemy is sin. Sin separates us from each other and from God. The one and only goal we have in the game of life is to find unity with God and others. We call this unity love. Through love God overcame sin and death and allowed us to find unity with him and others.

Life isn't pointless. Life is no simulation. Life is about accepting the love of God and overcoming the temptation to sin and separate ourselves from him. It is about building relationships with our neighbors (real, not simulated) so that we can grow in understanding the meaning of love.

CHAPTER 11
HYRULE OF HEAVEN

Nintendo was originally founded in 1889 by Fusajiro Yamauchi, not as a video game company but as a playing card company. The name *Nintendo* is said to mean "leave luck to heaven." Those who play video games, especially at a young age, might describe their experience exactly like living in heaven. We get to forget ourselves and our lives and experience the joy of another life.

Humans lost the experience of paradise because of Original Sin. We no longer live in a Garden of Eden, yet we are destined to live in another paradise. This is the essential message of Christianity. There is a God in heaven, and we are meant to be there with him.

The great Nintendo game designer, Shigeru Miyamoto, once described Hyrule—the world in which *The Legend of Zelda* series is set—as "a miniature garden that you can put into a drawer and revisit anytime you like."[1] In some ways, it is like a new Garden of Eden. Exploring Hyrule (despite its dangers) gives us the sense of awe and wonder. It is this same feeling that we get exploring all the games we grow to love.

Jesus Christ preached one consistent message throughout his life on earth. He described the promised kingdom of heaven that someone would give up an entire life to experience. "The kingdom of heaven is like treasure hidden in a field, which someone found and hid; then in his joy he goes and sells all that he has and buys that field" (Matthew 13:44). There is nothing more important than the kingdom. This is the gospel message. This is the good news he shared with those who came to listen to him.

As we live banished from the paradise of Eden, we also look forward in hope to the coming kingdom of heaven. If we love to explore Hyrule, just wait for the great joy of the true heavenly kingdom. When Jesus taught his disciples to pray, he told them to say "May your kingdom come. May your will be done on earth as it is in heaven" (Matthew 6:10). The kingdom of heaven is here. Go search for it among those who love the Lord.

CHAPTER 12
GAME OVER

The video game arcade was the central location of early gaming in the 1970s and '80s. In the arcade you play until your game is over. Every "Game Over" screen meant putting in another quarter to play again. At the most basic level, the goal of all video games is to keep playing. You must avoid the Game Over screen at all costs.

In many games Game Over means death. Fall in a pit, get eaten by a monster, or shot by a bad guy and the game is over. Just don't die and you keep playing.

Similarly, at the most basic level, the goal of life is to keep living. We use fight-or-flight instincts to protect ourselves from harm or death. Death in life is the ultimate Game Over.

Christianity gives us hope in the Game Over. During the video game of life, God's mercy gives us unlimited extra lives to keep playing. We suffer little deaths but rise again from our mistakes to carry on.

The message of Christianity is simple: Christ overcame life's Game Over. Through Jesus Christ's death and resurrection, we find hope in our own resurrection. There is a game after Game Over. The joys of heaven await those who turn to God and remain close to him.

To put it in another way, Jesus Christ paid a quarter for us to continue playing. In the arcade we eventually run out of quarters and can't play again. But in life Christ died and paid for us to keep playing. He has unlimited quarters for you to use if you turn to him during this life.

CHAPTER 13
EXTRA LIFE

In most video games, even though you die, you still have an extra life. You rise and try again. You also get opportunities to earn more extra lives as the games go on. Find the right power-up, earn enough coins, get the 1-up, or score enough points and you get an extra life.

An extra life is at the core of Christianity. Christian salvation means we get an extra life in heaven after we die. We also gain a new life in this world through baptism. We go into the waters dying to ourselves and come out of the waters reborn as a new child of God.

But we don't earn our extra lives through experience or accumulation of coins. We cannot find the hidden treasure to give us another life. This extra life was already earned for you. You cannot earn it yourself.

The way that this extra life was earned is pretty incredible. Jesus Christ had a life. God himself took on a human life, but gave it up. He died so that we could have an extra life. It would be like Mario running into a Goomba to give Luigi an extra life. Jesus Christ died so we could live.

Don't take this for granted. Through God's selfless act of love, he gives us another life. Don't waste it.

CHAPTER 14
FIND YOUR FATHER

Fallout is a series of postapocalyptic role-playing games set in a world ravaged by nuclear war. The main player characters in each installment of the series emerge from their fallout-shelter vaults to explore the wasteland above.

In the first two *Fallout*s, the protagonists are sent out to save their people, but the third installment gets more personal. In *Fallout 3*, which was developed by Bethesda Games in 2008, the goal of the game is to find your father amid the wasteland of Washington, DC. The opening scene of the game depicts the birth of the player character and the meeting between child and father. Then through a series of scenes in the vault the relationship continues to develop through childhood until, years later, the father disappears.

Why does the story line in this game touch our hearts so deeply? Jesus taught us to call God *Father*. "Pray then in this way: Our Father . . ." (Matthew 6:9). Hidden within our deepest longing is a desire to return to the Father. Just as the player character in *Fallout 3* leaves home to search for a father, so too do we grow up searching for our Father in heaven. (Is it any coincidence that the voice of the father in *Fallout 3* is none other than Liam Neeson, who also voiced the divine character of Aslan in *The Chronicles of Narnia*?)

Jesus spoke a lot about the journey to the Father, especially in the Gospel of John. "I am going to the Father," he said to his disciples (John 16:10). "I came from the Father and have come into the world; again, I am leaving the world and am going to the Father" (John 16:28). Jesus Christ showed us the way to the Father.

It's easy to wander aimlessly through life. You can wander without a purpose through the wasteland of *Fallout 3*, but the story only develops as you search for the father. Likewise, our journey develops as we follow Jesus. "You know the way to the place where I am going," Jesus said, "I am the way, and the truth, and the life" (John 14:4, 6).

Go out of your comfort zone and find your Father. Life will be more complex than this simple goal. Leaving the safety of the fallout shelter to find the father in *Fallout 3* leads to new missions and a greater purpose. As you search for God the Father in this life, your purpose will expand to a greater service of those around you. This deeper meaning and purpose, however, will always remain grounded in the love of God the Father.

Now let's learn more about this Father—and the Son and the Holy Spirit.

PART TWO
GOD

CHAPTER 15
THE MYST OF GOD

A puzzle game called *Myst* was the most popular computer game in the early 1990s. *Myst* is short for "mystery." In the game players travel through a book to a strange island called Myst. They must solve a series of puzzles in order to return home. Through beautiful imagery and thought-provoking clues, a fascinating backstory develops. Players click on and drag items to unlock new areas to explore. Once the entire island is explored and puzzles are solved, players come to a climactic end to the story.

Christians use the term "mystery" a lot. God is a mystery. The Trinity is a mystery. Christ's divinity is a mystery. Christ's death and resurrection is a mystery.

We use this term not to say that these concepts are so mysterious we cannot and should not understand them. This would mean never asking questions about God. It would mean blind acceptance of surface-level ideas rather than the faithful pursuit of truth.

As Christians, we are disciples. We are called to constantly learn. Disciples seek to uncover the mystery of God, seeking new clues and new understanding along the way.

Like the clues players unlock in *Myst*, a Christian seeks to unlock the clues to the Christian life. They come to know God in new ways every day as they uncover new aspects of the mystery. They grow in appreciation and understanding of the mystery of God. As they grow and study and learn, new and wonderful ways of seeing the world are unlocked. We continue to search and explore until one day all is revealed and we will see God face to face in heaven.

CHAPTER 16
A TRUE TRIFORCE

Beginning in the original NES (Nintendo Entertainment System) *The Legend of Zelda* (1986) and continuing in many of the Zelda sequels, the main character Link must collect pieces of the Triforce to complete the game. Once assembled, the Triforce appears as three equilateral triangles to form one large triangle. Find the Triforce, then save the princess and restore peace to Hyrule.

The Zelda series has its own mythological background by which the Triforce represents a balance in the world. Unite the Triforce and restore the balance. The inspiration for the image itself came from the Hojo clan of medieval Japan combined with some history of medieval Europe.

The triangle has been used as a symbol in Christian history because God is a Trinity of three persons: Father, Son, and Holy Spirit. Christians have represented the Trinity with many symbols, including a triangle, a shamrock, three intersecting circles, a triquetra (Trinity knot), and the fleur-de-lis.

Like Link, our goal in life is to find our own Triforce: the Trinity. To be a Christian is to be in a relationship with God. That relationship is expressed in a connection to all three persons of the Trinity. Our lives as Christians are defined by our encounters with God the Father, Jesus Christ the Son, and the Holy Spirit. Just as Link needs to find all the pieces of the Triforce, so too must we seek to cultivate a relationship with all three persons of the Trinity. Following the instructions of Jesus, all Christians have been baptized "in the name of the Father and of the Son and of the Holy Spirit" (Matthew 28:19).

It is important to ask ourselves how we think about and relate to each person of the Trinity, but it is also important to see the Trinity as one. It is like the three triangles of the Triforce united as one whole triangle. God as a Trinity of three persons exists in an eternal relationship of love. This love is poured forth into our lives and manifested in the way we love one another. God is not three separate beings. God is one being expressed in a relationship of three persons.

It is not easy to comprehend, but the image of the Triforce helps. God is one but also three. The Triforce is one but also three. They exist in a balance that gives life to the world.

CHAPTER 17
ICARUS AND ANGELS

Kid Icarus is a classic Nintendo video game series. The main character, Pit, with his angel-like wings and cupid-like arrows, eventually evolved into a sword-wielding fighter in *Super Smash Brothers*. Pit lives in the fantasy world Angel Land, but the character is based more on Greco-Roman mythology than Judeo-Christian angels. Pit is a combination of the mythological figures of Icarus and Cupid (Eros), but he looks a lot like a Christian angel.

To a Christian, angels are not myths. Angels are real, and angels work among us today. Throughout the Bible they are often praising God in heaven or bringing messages from the Lord to his people. The word "angel," in fact, comes from the Greek word *angelos*, which means "messenger."

While artistic representations of Christian angels might look a lot like the angels in *Kid Icarus*, they are not the same. Angels do not have bodies. They may have appeared like humans in the Bible, but they are pure spirit. Like us they have free will and the ability to turn away from God. Indeed, Satan and the demons are fallen angels who rejected God to find a place far from him in hell.

Yet the image of a fighting Kid Icarus is quite similar to a scene in the book of Revelation (12:7–9). A war broke out in heaven, and Saint Michael the Archangel led an army of angels against Satan, the great dragon and serpent, who was cast out of heaven along with his fallen angels. This is why Saint Michael the Archangel is often shown wielding a sword, like Pit in *Kid Icarus*.

The angels throughout the Bible and today remain God's servants. Some sing praise to him in heaven, but others watch over us and guard and guide us. Each of us has an angel watching over us. As Jesus explained, "Take care that you do not despise one of these little ones, for I tell you, in heaven their angels continually see the face of my Father in heaven" (Matthew 18:10). We call these angels guardian angels. We can find comfort in knowing an angel protects us with the skill and strength of Kid Icarus.

CHAPTER 18
CHRISTIANITY'S KILLER APP

Video game consoles almost always become popular because of the success of a single game. These games are called "system sellers" because people buy the entire gaming system to play a single game. If a particular company has exclusive access to a game, then players have no choice but to buy the entire console. This same phenomenon occurs in computers too, which have historically sold at high prices for single applications or "killer apps" (like spreadsheets for the Apple II).

Every popular video game system has its system sellers. People bought the original NES to play *Super Mario Bros.* and *The Legend of Zelda* (in its golden cartridge). Sega Genesis earned market share from Nintendo in the early nineties through exclusive access to *Sonic the Hedgehog*, *John Madden Football*, and the uncensored version of *Mortal Kombat*. People upgraded from NES to the SNES to play *Street Fighter II* and *Donkey Kong Country*. PlayStation won the late-nineties console wars with system sellers like *Tekken*, *Tomb Raider*, *Crash Bandicoot*, and ultimately *Final Fantasy VII*. Then Nintendo 64 earned back popularity with *Mario Kart 64* and *GoldenEye 007*. Kids played these games at their friends' houses or saw commercials on TV that led them to convince their parents to buy an entire new gaming system.

Just as every successful video game console has a system seller, imagine what Christianity's system seller might be. What leads a person to accept an entire religion despite early doubts and controversial mistakes from Christian leaders or peers? The answer might sound obvious, but dig a little deeper.

Jesus Christ is Christianity's system seller. When people authentically encounter the person of Jesus Christ and begin to form relationship with him, they start to accept all that comes with him. In the gospels people are drawn to Jesus because they know he can heal them. Again and again stories about Jesus's healing miracles show not only the physical healing but a much more important spiritual healing from sin. "Which is easier, to say, 'Your sins are forgiven,' or to say, 'Stand up and walk'?" (Matthew 9:5). A relationship with Jesus leads to the forgiveness of sins.

Today we can encounter Jesus Christ through the Church. When a Christian community is welcoming and an example of the unconditional love of Jesus Christ, then new people see his light and want to learn more about Jesus Christ themselves. People don't convert to Christianity because of perfect Christians. They convert because they see a Christian's relationship with Christ. If these new potential Christians were to rely on the people in the Christian community, they would undoubtedly be disappointed. Jesus Christ is always the system seller. We accept all that comes with Christianity so that we can have access to him.

CHAPTER 19
GOD OR DEMIGOD?

Final Fantasy VI (better known as *Final Fantasy III* on the SNES in the United States) opens with a mysterious character named Terra. In a world where magic is mostly a myth, Terra can cast spells without technology. During the game it is later revealed that the green-haired heroine is half-human, half-esper. Espers were godlike beings whose presence brought magic into the world.

Half-gods are called demigods in Western mythology. Their names might be familiar: Heracles, Achilles, Dionysus, Orion, Perseus, and Theseus. The *God of War* video game series was inspired by the pantheon of Greek gods and features a demigod named Kratos as its main character. Kratos had a god as a father and a human as a mother.

Jesus Christ had a human mother and a divine Father, but he was not half-man, half-god. Unlike Terra, Kratos, and other demigods, Jesus was fully human and fully divine. This difference is what makes Jesus Christ unique. During the early centuries after Jesus died and rose again, Christians in the Church spent many years trying to verbalize this essential truth about Jesus's nature.

Ultimately, the Church's leaders met in ecumenical councils to find the best terms to use to distinguish Jesus as fully God and fully man. They crafted the now well-known Nicene Creed, in which we declare Jesus Christ is "the Only Begotten Son of God, born of the Father before all ages. God from God, Light from Light, true God from true God, begotten, not made, consubstantial with the Father; through him all things were made." Then we continue the creed by recounting the story of the annunciation in Luke, saying, "He came down from heaven, and by the Holy Spirit was incarnate of the Virgin Mary."[1]

Jesus was no demigod. He was more than a superhero human with special powers, and he was not less than God. He was God and he was also a man. He is "Emmanuel," which means "God is with us." This makes his sacrifice on the cross all the more important. "Though he existed in the form of God, did not regard equality with God as something to be grasped, but emptied himself, taking the form of a slave, assuming human likeness. . . . He humbled himself and became obedient to the point of death—even death on a cross" (Philippians 2:6–8).

Jesus Christ died for us. He gave up his life so that we could have life as one of God's children. As Saint Athanasius put it, "The Son of God became man so that man might become God."[2]

CHAPTER 20
CHRIST THE CHOSEN ONE

The main character in many fantasy books, movies, and video games often fulfills a chosen-one prophecy. Harry Potter, Luke Skywalker in *Star Wars*, Paul Atreides in *Dune*, and Neo in *The Matrix* are some of the best known "chosen ones" in books and movies. Their story lines fulfilled ancient prophecies to restore peace and balance to the world.

Video games have their fair share of chosen ones as well. The main character in the *Secret of Mana* on the SNES was a chosen one. The main character in *Dragon Quest* is a descendant of a great hero with many of the common chosen-one traits. The heroes in *Elder Scrolls* are related to the prophecies in the elder scrolls, and the player character in *Skyrim* is blessed with the immortal soul of a dragon. The player character in *Fallout 2* even goes by the literal title "Chosen One" as the descendant of the hero in the first game of the series.

Each of these many chosen-one characters falls into a similar pattern inspired by the coming of Jesus Christ. Jesus was the "chosen one" who fulfilled the prophecies about the Messiah in the Old Testament. In fact, "Christ" is not Jesus's last name but the Greek translation of the word *Messiah. Christ* means "Messiah," which means "Anointed One."

The disciples who met Jesus at the beginning of the Gospel of John were filled with joy. Andrew proclaimed to his brother Peter, "'We have found the Messiah' (which is translated Anointed)" (John 1:41). When put to the test in the other gospels, Jesus asks Peter who he says that Jesus is, and Peter responds, "You are the Messiah, the Son of the living God" (Matthew 16:16).

This was an incredible realization. For centuries the Jews looked forward to the coming of the Messiah, the Chosen One. Jesus Christ was that Chosen One. He would come to restore peace in the world. He would heal the sick and raise us from the dead. All would be fulfilled in the one, true Chosen One.

CHAPTER 21
WHERE IN THE WORLD IS JESUS CHRIST?

"Do it Rockapella!" Kids who grew up in the 1990s will remember this catchy jingle as if it were yesterday and sing: "Where in the world is Carmen Sandiego?" But before it was a 1990s TV show on PBS and a Netflix series in the 2020s, *Carmen Sandiego* was an early edutainment video game on the computer beginning in 1985. As they played the game, kids would learn geography and history while searching for the criminal mastermind, Carmen Sandiego.

In the game (and show) the Chief from ACME Detective Agency hired players as gumshoes to locate and apprehend Carmen's henchmen (with funny names like Hardley Worthit, Rob M. Blind, Patty Larceny, Sarah Nade, and others) and ultimately Carmen Sandiego herself using various clues along the worldwide trail. Players searched for Carmen in amazing places from Argentina to Australia, Peking to Parish, Kathmandu to Istanbul, London, Rome, Tokyo, and more.

Imagine if there were a similar game about locating the Son of God, Jesus Christ. Where in the world is the Son of

God? Well, God chose to make himself known to a small and relatively unknown people. "It was not because you were more numerous than any other people that the LORD set his heart on you and chose you, for you were the fewest of all peoples. It was because the LORD loved you and kept the oath that he swore to your ancestors" (Deuteronomy 7:7–8).

The people of Israel escaped from the powerful kingdom in Egypt to establish their own home in Canaan. They were small in number and remained relatively small compared to the great powers that surrounded them. They were conquered many times and even sent into exile to live away from their home and capital city of Jerusalem. Eventually they were able to return and establish themselves in Jerusalem again, but by the time Jesus was born, the Jewish people were living under the rule of the Roman Empire. The Jews were a relatively small group of people compared to other parts of the vast empire.

Yet God chose to come into the world in this unlikely location. Jesus was born in the small town of Bethlehem outside of Jerusalem. He grew up in Nazareth, a backwoods and easily overlooked location. He died in Jerusalem under an insignificant Roman governor, Pontius Pilate.

This is the setting through which God revealed himself to the world. It fits with the messages Jesus taught to his disciples. "The last will be first, and the first will be last" (Matthew 20:16). "All who exalt themselves will be humbled, and all who humble themselves will be exalted" (Matthew 23:12). Skilled gumshoes would never expect the Son of God to appear in such humble beginnings, and yet that was exactly God's plan.

CHAPTER 22
LEVEL 1 LORD

In life and in video games we all start out at level 1. As infants we have no skills or experience. Our parents must help us grow and learn. With their help and the help of others, we increase in size and ability, like a character increases in levels.

It's remarkable to even imagine, but our God was born into this world as a baby, like you and me. To put it in terms of a video game, our God came into the world at level 1. He was still divine, of course, but also human. He wasn't born able to walk or talk or do the things that adults could do.

Many of us know the story of Christmas and the birth of Christ, but it is worth remembering once more. Mary and Joseph traveled to Bethlehem and there was no room for them anywhere to stay, not even in the inn. Therefore God himself was born in a manger, which is a feeding trough for animals. Our Level 1 Lord started with nothing. He was born into poverty.

What's the message? With these humble beginnings, God expressed the prophecies by Isaiah and fulfilled them in Jesus Christ. "Look, the virgin shall become pregnant and give birth to a son, and they shall name him Emmanuel, which means, 'God is with us'" (Matthew 1:23). Again, in terms of video games, Jesus Christ began his life at level 1 just like every one of us.

God could have come into the world as a level 99 fully divine being. Yet instead, he chose to be fully divine and also fully human. As a human he started at the lowest level just like us. Yet even this Level 1 Lord deserved glory and praise. The angels appeared to shepherds in the fields on the day of his birth, singing, "Glory to God in the highest heaven, and on earth peace among those whom he favors" (Luke 2:14). The shepherds came to see the child and gave God glory and praise. Likewise, magi coming from the East came to pay respects as well, for this young boy deserved to be paid homage.

CHAPTER 23
THE CARPENTER

Nintendo's Mario is a classic everyman character. He became the perfect mascot for the Nintendo company not for his impressive physique or heroic backstory, but for his relatability. He is just an ordinary guy doing extraordinary things.

While most of us think of Mario as a plumber, his original career was a carpenter. In Nintendo's first hit arcade game *Donkey Kong* (1981), Mario appears as "Jumpman," climbing up ladders and jumping over Donkey Kong's barrels. He can also smash obstacles with a hammer. The game takes place in a construction site with a familiar goal: rescue the damsel in distress.

Jesus Christ was also a carpenter, of course. Think about the importance of this. God became man and spent most of his life building things as an ordinary carpenter. This profession and ordinary life make Jesus relatable. He became like one of us. Just like we find it easier to relate to Mario as a carpenter, so too can we find a mutual connection with the Son of God, Jesus Christ.

Who would have predicted a carpenter in red overalls would become one of the most recognizable characters in history? Who would have predicted a carpenter from a small town in Galilee would become the most recognizable name in history? A simple profession and a heroic adventure of salvation combine to change the world.

CHAPTER 24
HEALING SPRING OF BAPTISM

There are many ways to regain life in video games, ranging from potions to health packs to various kinds of foods. Among these is the healing spring, a common trope in video games. You will find them in the *Final Fantasy* series, *Breath of Fire* series, *The Legend of Zelda* series, and *World of Warcraft*, among others.

This trope is inspired, in part, by the influence of Christian baptism. Not only was Jesus baptized, but he also commanded his apostles to go and "make disciples of all nations, baptizing them in the name of the Father and of the Son and of the Holy Spirit" (Matthew 28:19).

In Christian baptism we do not experience a renewal of physical health, but we are restored. Our souls are cleansed of sin and we are reborn as God's sons and daughters. Just as God the Father identified Jesus as his "beloved Son" during his baptism, so too do we identify as God's children.

Christians are only baptized with water once, but the holy water within churches reminds us of our baptisms. It reminds us of the healing power of the Lord to remove the stain of sin so we can truly live up to our potential as adopted children of God.

As Christians we lead people to the healing waters of baptism. We welcome them into God's chosen people by showing them the way to the Lord. Echo the words spoken by Ananias, who invited Saint Paul to be baptized, saying, "Why do you delay? Get up, be baptized, and have your sins washed away, calling on his name." (Acts 22:16).

CHAPTER 25
JOEL 3:16

John 3:16 might be the most popular verse in the Bible. It has often been displayed on signs at sporting events and on billboards along the side of the highway. It comes from a conversation between Jesus and a man named Nicodemus about salvation. Jesus said, "For God so loved the world that he gave his only Son, so that everyone who believes in him may not perish but may have eternal life" (John 3:16).

Those who have heard this verse many times may not fully appreciate how heartbreaking this gift really was for God the Father. God was willing to lose his only Son to death. He watched him suffer. He watched him die.

We get a taste of this pain in the popular video game *The Last of Us*. Made exclusively for PlayStation 3, *The Last of Us* is one of the highest rated games in history and ranked among the best of all time. It comes as no surprise that the TV adaptation of the game on HBO became such a hit. The gameplay is great, but like many modern video games, it is the characters and story line that players find compelling.

In the game's prologue, the player controls the main character Joel's daughter, Sarah, on the night of a terrible zombie outbreak. Joel and his brother try to get Sarah out of the city as chaos erupts all around them. Joel manages to save Sarah from the zombie-like "infected" people and nearly manages to escape. Then in a heart-wrenching encounter with a soldier trying to maintain a quarantine of all people within the city, Sarah is shot. She dies in Joel's arms, and the real game begins.

Twenty years later and Joel has spiraled into the life of a smuggler. He is distant and unhappy. Then he is hired to transport a young girl named Ellie across the country. She is immune to the pandemic that ravaged the world. If Joel can keep her safe and successfully complete the journey, he might be able to save the world.

Think about the similarities to the Bible verse John 3:16. Joel lost his child but must save another. The differences, however, are important. God loved his Son with an even greater love than Joel had for his daughter. God also loved all other people, including those who were responsible for his Son's death. God loved the world. He did not spiral into anger. He did not punish the world for killing his child.

God willingly gave up his Son for us, and today God helps us become one of his children. He is with us. He helps us. He protects us from harm as we travel along our journeys of life. He will do everything to make sure we are saved along with the rest of the human race.

CHAPTER 26
PREACHING IN SIDE QUESTS

Many modern video games (especially RPGs) have side quests that players can choose to complete while they play. These side quests are not part of the larger mission or story line of the game, but they often enable players to learn something new about their characters or uncover unique items. These side quests are like smaller stories within the larger story line of the game.

The gospels are full of side quests for Christians to read today. Jesus Christ preached in a set of side quests that we call parables. A parable is an earthly story that teaches a heavenly lesson. Jesus's parables give us insights into who Jesus is and what he has to offer the world. Jesus's life and death established the kingdom of heaven, but his parables helped people understand what that kingdom is actually like.

In the Parable of the Prodigal Son, for example, we can imagine ourselves as a sinful son returning to a loving father. In the Parable of the Good Samaritan, we learn the meaning of love and mercy compared to self-right-eousness. In the short Parable of the Hidden Treasure, we come to understand that the value of God's kingdom is more important than every other possession we own.

The parables are side quests worthy of our attention. Reading them and meditating on their words, by putting ourselves in the story, will help us understand the larger story of Jesus's life, death, and resurrection. These parables can be enjoyable stories to explore and unlock new parts of ourselves and our relationship with Jesus Christ.

CHAPTER 27
DEATH BY DYSENTERY

Every child of the 1980s remembers the many failed attempts to travel from Independence, Missouri, to Oregon on a computer . *The Oregon Trail* was the earliest and most popular form of video game edutainment. It was a video game, but also a way to teach kids nineteenth-century United States history. Most schools in the eighties had the game installed in their computer labs for students to play during classes and free time.

The journey on the Oregon Trail is treacherous. Food and supplies dwindle as players try to keep the traveling party healthy. Players can choose to hunt and play a mini-game to shoot deer, buffalo, and other animals for food to feed their children. They must ford rivers or pay the toll of a ferry.

Always there remains the growing fear of death on the trail. Party members die from drowning, snakebites, exhaustion, cholera, fever, and many other diseases, but most memorably they fear the screen that says, "You have died of dysentery."

One of Jesus's primary activities on earth was to heal the sick. He healed people of their diseases almost everywhere he went. With the advances in modern medicine, the fear of illness is less prevalent today than in the past. Most people don't even know what dysentery is. (Trust me, you don't want to know.) Nevertheless, today we still suffer from the unpredictability of illnesses like cancer, heart disease, and dementia.

Very few kids in the 1980s ever beat *The Oregon Trail*. Most died along the way. The game seemed impossible and hopeless, especially once party members got sick. Imagine if Jesus Christ was in the game. It would have been a lot easier to reach the destination. Jesus the healer offers hope for the hopeless. He comes to us when we live in fear or need him the most.

Sickness and disease can cause hopelessness because they are something we cannot control. Think about the other ways in which a lack of control over our lives leads to hopelessness. This is exactly where Jesus wants to meet us. For when we are weak, then we are strong, as Saint Paul wrote to the Corinthians (2 Corinthians 12:10).

CHAPTER 28
TRANSFIGURATION: CHRIST'S CROSSOVER EVENT

The transfiguration was a significant turning point in the gospel story of Jesus's life. He took three of his disciples (Peter, James, and John) up a mountain. There he was raised up in the sky with clothes like light with two important figures appearing next to him. On one side was Moses, who'd led God's people out of Israel and through whom God gave the Israelites the Law. On the other side was Elijah, the great prophet of the Old Testament who some thought would return to earth from heaven. Through this event the Lord showed that Jesus was the fulfillment of both the Law (Moses) and the Prophets (Elijah) of the Old Testament.

It was the Bible's great crossover event. There have been many video games featuring characters that cross over from multiple games. Nintendo has its two major successes in crossover games with the *Mario Kart* series and *Super Smash Bros.* series. In the latter, classic characters from different games, like Mario, Link, Samus, Star Fox, and Pikachu, face off against each other. Later variations of the game include an even greater selection of characters to choose from, including Cloud and Sephiroth from *Final Fantasy VII* and Steve from *Minecraft*.

Fortnite Battle Royale has been known for its crossover events featuring characters outside of video games. Often these events align with the release of real-world happenings or movies. Crossover events have featured characters from *Star Wars* to Marvel to DC Comics and even to professional sports, like football and soccer.

In many ways the transfiguration in the New Testament was more than just a crossover event. The key moment of the story was when the disciples heard a voice from the clouds saying, "This is my Son, the Beloved; listen to him" (Mark 9:7). This would be like a video game crossover event in which players were told that the one crossover character was more important than all the others. Jesus is more than just an important figure in the Bible. Jesus Christ is God's son. While gamers could debate the most important character ever created in a game, there is no doubt that Jesus Christ is the most important person ever to walk the earth.

Heed the words that the disciples heard on the mountain. Jesus Christ is God's son. Listen to him.

CHAPTER 29
SIMCITY OF DAVID

Before *The Sims* and the many spinoffs in the Sims series (*SimEarth*, *SimAnt*, and *SimTower*, among others) came the classic game *SimCity* (1989). *SimCity* is an open-ended game in which players build (as the title suggests) a simulated city. Players decide how to manage the development of the city in real time, adding residential areas, commercial buildings, utilities, and public service buildings to attract new citizens and keep current citizens happy. Believe it or not, the game made urban planning fun.

God did his own sort of urban planning with his people in the Old Testament, to develop the city of Jerusalem. Originally, Jerusalem was ruled by various groups of Canaanites before King David defeated the Jebusites and made their capital city his own. Most importantly, however, King David brought the Ark of the Covenant into the city to establish it as the center of worship for the people of Israel. This is why the city of Jerusalem has also been called the City of David.

Unfortunately, Jerusalem and the Israelites had a difficult history. After David's son King Solomon died, the kingdom of Israel was divided into two kingdoms: Israel in the North and Judah in the South. Both kingdoms struggled to defend themselves against foreign powers. First, the Northern Kingdom fell in 722 BC, then Judah fell in 587 BC. Like the monsters of the arcade game *Rampage* (1986), the great powers of the North destroyed the city, and the people were sent into exile.

Eventually the people of Judah (now called the Jews) returned to the city. They never quite kept their independence though. They were eventually conquered and ruled by the Roman Empire. The Romans ruled over Jerusalem and the Jews during the life of Jesus Christ.

If Jerusalem were built in *SimCity*, then the most important structure to build for the people would be the Temple. King Solomon built the Temple and placed the Ark of the Covenant within it. It became the central location for worship. The Temple was destroyed each time the city was conquered, much to the horror of God's people.

Therefore, when Jesus said to "destroy this temple, and in three days I will raise it up" (John 2:19), the people were rightfully shocked. They had repeatedly been rebuilding it for centuries. But Jesus was not referring to the actual temple—he was referring to his body. His body was the new temple and the new center of worship for God's people.

In Jerusalem Jesus would suffer, die, and rise from the dead. Matthew's gospel reminds us of Jesus's words about destroying the temple and rebuilding it in three days, with accusations from the people witnessing his death. But again, he was talking about his body. When Jesus Christ died, Matthew tells us that the earth shook and "at that moment the curtain of the temple was torn in two, from top to bottom" (Matthew 27:51).

From that moment forward, Jesus was the center of worship for Christians. They no longer needed the Temple in Jerusalem. Jesus was the temple. Christianity then spread not just in the old kingdom of Israel but far and wide to all kingdoms throughout the world. The worship continued to spread throughout history and will continue until the day Jesus establishes a New Jerusalem "coming down out of heaven from God [with] the glory of God and a radiance like a very rare jewel, like jasper, clear as crystal" (Revelation 21:10–11). There will be no temple in the new Jerusalem "for its temple is the Lord God the Almighty and the Lamb" (Revelation 21:22).

CHAPTER 30
MANNA (NOT MANA) FROM HEAVEN

Magic power is often referred to as "mana" in video games. Mana points are equivalent to magic points in many RPGs. Usually when you cast a spell in a game, you must spend mana points. You must replenish your mana again to cast more spells.

The term *mana* can be traced back through some fantasy short stories and novels of the 1970s. It is also a term used in Oceanian mythology to refer to spiritual energy or life force. It often had a healing power to it as well.

No video game popularized the word mana more than Square's SNES classic *Secret of Mana* (1993). The game begins, "Darkness sweeps the troubled land, as mana's power fades. . . . People await a hero who will wield the sword . . . the sword of mana." The game's plot is based on the fear of humanity using up all the mana to create the *Mana Fortress* warship. In the game the players must take on the evil empire as it seeks to locate and protect the eight Mana Seeds that would power the *Mana Fortress* and drain the world's life energy.

Mana (one "n") is different from manna (two "n's") in the Bible. In the Old Testament God sent down bread from heaven to feed the Israelites in the desert. They called this bread "manna," which is based on the Hebrew word for "gift" (Exodus 16). Unlike mana in video games, the manna did not give the Israelites spiritual power or life energy. The bread was meant to physically sustain them. It was food given so that they would not starve.

Many centuries later, however, Jesus Christ explained to his disciples that he was the new manna from heaven. He came so that God's people would have everlasting life. "Your ancestors ate the manna in the wilderness," he said, "and they died. . . . I am the living bread that came down from heaven. Whoever eats of this bread will live forever, and the bread that I will give for the life of the world is my flesh" (John 6:49, 51).

We believe that Christ is the heavenly manna. Manna and mana are very different. The purpose of manna is to give us everlasting life. Jesus Christ gives us everlasting life. He does not give us magic mana points to use for special powers. This manna can never be used up because Jesus Christ is everlasting. The manna that he gives is for the life of the world. It can never be drained or used for evil.

CHAPTER 31
THE LAST SUPER SUPPER

What makes Mario and Luigi super in the *Super Mario Bros.* video game series? The power-ups, of course! Power-ups are common in video games, and in many games, food is the main source of power-ups. Characters become super by eating mushrooms, flowers, fruit, cake, pizza, rations, and many other foods and drinks.

The word *super* means "especially," "very good," or "excellent." It comes from the Latin word *super*, which means "above" or "beyond."

The word *supper* has a similar sound but a different meaning. It comes from an Old French word meaning to "sup" or "to dip bread in wine." A supper is an evening meal.

Jesus shared an evening meal of bread and wine with his disciples. We call this event the Last Supper. During the meal, Jesus said something quite shocking. On the night before he died, he took bread and gave thanks saying, "This is my body that is for you. Do this in remembrance of me" (1 Corinthians 11:24). In a similar way, he took the cup of wine and said, "This cup is the new covenant in my blood. Do this, as often as you drink it, in remembrance of me." (1 Corinthians 11:25).

From that point forward Christians have been gathering on Sundays for the breaking of bread in remembrance of Jesus Christ and the Last Supper. This bread and wine may not give us special powers of invincibility or throwing fireballs, but they do make us super. Within the bread and wine, Jesus himself is revealed to us. As the disciples on the road to Emmaus experienced: "He had been made known to them in the breaking of the bread" (Luke 24:35). So, too, is Jesus made known to us in the communal celebration of the breaking of the bread. What makes the Last Supper so super? It isn't the special powers—it is the way in which we remember Jesus and how he makes himself present to us.

CHAPTER 32
JUDAS AMONG US

At the beginning of the game *Among Us*, players are randomly chosen to be either Crewmates or Imposters. The Crewmates must identify and eject the Imposters or complete all their assigned tasks. The Imposters secretly plot to kill the Crewmates before they complete their assigned tasks. Imposters must blend in to win the game. They must appear to be loyal members of the crew so that everyone else on the ship believes them to be innocent.

The players meet during a group meeting to identify and eject the Imposters. They vote to decide who will be ejected based on the testimonies of the players. Crewmates make their case based on evidence they have observed. Imposters lie to conceal their identities.

Jesus held a similar meeting at the Last Supper. "Truly I tell you, one of you will betray me" (Matthew 26:21). His followers were distressed and in shock. "Surely not I, Lord?" they said in reply. Eleven knew they were loyal, but one was a liar. Judas Iscariot, one of Jesus's Twelve chosen apostles, would betray Jesus for thirty pieces of silver.

Jesus knew the identity of the imposter, but he didn't eject him. He didn't stop him. He allowed himself to be captured and later killed. When Judas came leading a large crowd of people to arrest Jesus, the other disciples deserted Jesus and ran away.

Are you a Christian Crewmate or Imposter? As Christians, we want to echo the words of the apostles, who said in shock, "Surely not I, Lord?" Yet we often fail to follow Jesus. We find ourselves watching Jesus suffer while we are afraid to suffer with him. Sometimes we might even choose money or recognition, like Judas, instead of the suffering that comes with being a disciple of the Lord.

CHAPTER 33
GARMENTS 'N GOBLINS

The arcade game *Ghosts 'n Goblins* by Capcom was a huge success and ported into home game consoles, along with its sequels, like *Ghouls 'n Ghosts*. Players control a medieval knight named Sir Arthur as he fights monsters, zombies, and giants on his way to defeat Astaroth, who is also called the Devil or Great Satan.

The game is difficult, and players can only be hit twice before dying. On the first hit, Sir Arthur loses his armor and must fight with a weaker weapon. He runs across the screen wearing only his undergarments. One more hit and he will die.

Jesus's battle against Satan has some similarities. Like Sir Arthur, Jesus was stripped of his garments. "When the soldiers had crucified Jesus, they took his clothes and divided them into four parts, one for each solider. . . . to fulfill what the scripture says, 'They divided my clothes among themselves, and for my clothing they cast lots'" (John 19:23–24). But unlike Sir Arthur, Jesus willingly allowed himself to be weak. To defeat the final boss, he did not use armor or the best weapons. Jesus lost everything to be nailed naked on the cross. He gave up his life and died so that we could be saved.

This is the great mystery of Jesus Christ's sacrifice. He did not seek power or strength but allowed himself to be beaten and killed. "He humbled himself and became obedient to the point of death—even death on a cross" (Philippians 2:8). *Ghosts 'n Goblins* is so much harder to play without the good weapons and the armor. It was harder for Jesus to be so weak before his death, yet that was the point. He gave up his life in humiliation so that we could live forever.

CHAPTER 34
THE SHEEP OF GOD

Among the most common mobs (mobile objects) wandering around the *Minecraft* universe are the sheep. They are the main source of wool and a good source of mutton for players to eat as well. Unlike the zombies and other hostile *Minecraft* mobs, the sheep wander innocently around the world. They do nothing wrong, yet players sacrifice them for materials they need to survive.

Sheep and lambs are mentioned often in the Bible. God's people are often described as a flock of sheep, with God as their shepherd. Even Jesus describes himself as the "Good Shepherd" (John 10:11, 14). But it was even more shocking when John the Baptist called Jesus the "Lamb of God."

It is possible to breed sheep and produce a lamb within *Minecraft*. They are small and cute little mobs, but killing them won't even produce wool. In the Old Testament killing a lamb as a sacrifice was important to the Israelites. In the book of Exodus, God told the Israelites to sacrifice an innocent lamb, then to spread the blood over the doors of their homes to protect them during the Passover. The sacrificial lamb enabled them to be freed from Egypt.

When John the Baptist identified Jesus as the "Lamb of God who takes away the sin of the world" in the beginning of John (1:29), a lot of eyebrows would have been raised. Not only would the Jews of Jesus's day remember the sacrificial Passover lamb, but they would also consider the words of the Prophet Isaiah, who described the coming suffering servant who "was wounded for our transgressions, crushed for our iniquities . . . like a lamb that is led to the slaughter" (Isaiah 53:5, 7).

Jesus Christ is our paschal (Passover) lamb, whose sacrifice enabled us to be free from sin. He was innocent like a little lamb and killed so that we could be free. He was slaughtered on a cross, and through him we have life.

When John saw Jesus in heaven in the Book of Revelation, he saw him in the form of a slain lamb. Around him a crowd of angels sang "worthy is the lamb that was slaughtered to receive power and wealth and wisdom and might and honor and glory and blessing!" (Revelation 5:12). Then the saints echoed these words and bowed down to worship him.

Can you imagine the sight? Imagine elevating an insignificant sheep from *Minecraft* as the very symbol for God himself! God did not appear in great power and might, but that is exactly how the angels and saints describe the Lamb of God in heaven. What an incredible expression of the humility of Jesus Christ and the humility he calls us to model as well.

Be humble like sheep. Follow the Good Shepherd. Be grateful for the incredible sacrifice of the Lamb of God so that we might enter into eternal life with the Lord in heaven.

CHAPTER 35
DEAD AND REDEMPTION

The main characters in the *Red Dead Redemption* series are gunslinging outlaws who need to make amends for past crimes. In *Red Dead Redemption*, players control John Marston, whose family is kidnapped by the Bureau of Investigation at the beginning of the game. Marston can get his family back in return for hunting down his former gang members.

Red Dead Redemption 2 is a prequel, taking place twenty years earlier than the events of *Red Dead Redemption*. As the outlaw Arthur Morgan, players must cooperate with the Van der Linde gang to earn enough loot to escape the outlaw life of the old Wild West and retire. Like the first installment in the series, the game includes a morality system that affects the story line and the ways the NPCs (non-player characters) interact. The overlying question is whether the outlaws in the game can maintain a code of honor while committing crimes and hunting down bad guys.

As Christians we hear the word *redemption* a lot. Redemption simply means to "buy back." You could redeem a prize you earned in an arcade with tickets. You can also redeem a debt you owe for a car or a house. In *Red Dead Redemption*, the outlaws attempt to redeem themselves to escape the criminal life.

Unlike the characters in *Red Dead Redemption*, Jesus Christ was not a criminal—yet he was sentenced to death as an outlaw. He was innocent of any crime; therefore, he had no debt to pay for the crimes he did not commit.

Yet Jesus Christ gave up his life to buy back our salvation. He was punished for a crime he did not commit and redeemed us by paying off our debt. Therefore, we don't have to earn back our debt before death. Jesus paid it off already. He redeemed us. "When you were dead in trespasses . . . God made you alive together with him, when he forgave us all our trespasses, erasing the record that stood against us with its legal demands," wrote Saint Paul (Colossians 2:13–14). What did he use as a form of payment? Saint Paul continued, "He set this aside, nailing it to the cross" (Colossians 2:14).

Unlike the outlaws in *Red Dead Redemption*, we don't have to earn our way out of the mistakes we have made. "In [Jesus Christ] we have redemption through his blood, the forgiveness of our trespasses, according to the riches of his grace" (Ephesians 1:7). He paid off our debt and redeemed us. Now we can live a life free from the guilt of sin—but always in gratitude to Christ for the sacrifice he made for us. Any mistake we make can be redeemed through the grace of Jesus Christ, who willingly gave up his life for us. His death led to our redemption.

CHAPTER 36
CONTROLLER CROSS

Video game controllers come in all shapes and sizes. Joysticks, modeled after the classic arcade controls, were the most common video game controllers in the 1970s and early '80s. As the original Nintendo Entertainment System rose in rapid popularity, so too did their D-pad (directional pad) video game controller.

The D-pad (or +Control Pad, as it is officially called by Nintendo) includes a directional pad in the shape of a cross to navigate up, down, left, right, and diagonally. Since the launch of the NES, nearly all major video game systems have included the D-pad cross design in their controllers. With the movement of their left thumb, players press a cross to move and interact with the game.

Including a cross in video game controllers was purely for a practical purpose—however, it functions as a nice reminder for Christians. There within your hands when playing a game is a cross. Jesus said to "take up your cross daily and follow me" (Luke 9:23). In a video game controller, we use this cross to move. "In him we live and move and have our being" (Acts 17:28), Paul preached to the Athenians. We move and live within the Cross.

Many Christians throughout history have worn or carried crosses with them as a reminder of this call to carry our spiritual crosses. As a gamer, take up the cross of your controller and choose to follow the path of Christ, who selflessly suffered and died for us. Are you willing to make similar self-sacrifices as a person and as a player today? You are called to carry a cross. Go out and seek to serve others in the way that the Lord is calling you to serve.

CHAPTER 37

RAIDING THE EMPTY TOMB

The story of Jesus Christ does not end in death. The Son of God died and was buried, but on the third day Mary Magdalene came to Jesus's tomb. She came with some other women followers of Jesus to anoint his body. In shock, however, they arrived to find the stone covering the entrance of the tomb had been removed and the tomb was empty!

Tomb Raider's Lara Croft visited her fair share of tombs as well. In each of the *Tomb Raider* video games, Croft explores tombs around the world, searching for "arte-facts." Players have fun adventures and solve interesting puzzles along the way.

Like Lara Croft, Mary Magdalene had a puzzle to solve. There was nothing to find in Jesus's tomb. In one version of the story, she ran to ask the apostles Peter and John to come see for themselves (John 20:1–10). In another version of the story, an angel appears to explain, "He is not here, for he has been raised, as he said" (Matthew 28:6).

The tomb was empty. Jesus had been raised from the dead, proving what he said was true. He died and redeemed humankind so that we might not die but have eternal life. "I am the resurrection and the life. Those who believe in me, even though they die, will live" (John 11:25).

Death is not the end for us either. "God raised the Lord and will also raise us by his power." (1 Corinthians 6:14). Jesus is not here. He has been raised and left the tomb, and his body is now with God the Father. He left this message for Mary Magdalene to share with the disciples, "I am ascending to my Father and your Father, to my God and your God" (John 20:17). We do not enter the tomb like Lara Croft, but rather, like Mary Magdalene, we leave the tomb and go out and proclaim the good news: He is risen!

CHAPTER 38
SAVED GAMES

In the early arcade video games, there was no need to save your progress. Arcade games were designed to be difficult so that players would have to use as many quarters as possible to play. As the at-home consoles rose in popularity and video games added longer gameplay and narrative elements, playing through an entire game in one sitting became increasingly impossible.

Cartridges for many video games were built with a memory space to save progress. Some games allowed you to pause and save at any time, while others required you to reach a certain save point. After the game was saved, you could die but start again at the save point as if the death never happened.

Christians talk about being saved a lot. Through Christ's death and resurrection, we are saved from sin. Salvation does not prevent death, just like saving a game does not make you invincible. But through Christ's salvation, we rise again with him.

It is important to remember that Jesus declined the opportunity to save himself. People scoffed at him. "He saved others; let him save himself if he is the Messiah of God, his chosen one" (Luke 23:35). Even the criminal next to him on a cross said, "Save yourself and us" (Luke 23:39). But he did not save his own life. He did not save his game. He died, but the game was not over.

Just as Jesus rose again, so too can we rise again, like a save point of a video game. Not only do we rise again with him in heaven, but we also get to experience a taste of salvation today. Through Jesus's sacrifice on the cross, we receive his mercy. We turn to him, asking for forgiveness, receive his mercy, and begin where we left off.

Will we be tempted to sin again? Yes, of course. Just like a player attempting to defeat a boss after a save point, we receive God's mercy and attempt to overcome the temptation and sin again. With God's grace and help, we can defeat the sin the next time.

CHAPTER 39
BLOW ON IT

The original Nintendo cartridges of the 1980s and '90s didn't work perfectly. Sometimes when you inserted the cartridge and turned on the power, the TV screen would not display the game correctly. Everyone knew what to do. Take the game out and blow on the bottom to get rid of dust and debris. Insert the game and try again. After a few tries, the games usually worked.

There is a striking similarity to breath in the Bible and blowing on NES cartridges. In Genesis God created Adam from the ground and "breathed into his nostrils the breath of life, and the man became a living being" (Genesis 2:7). We have to breathe to live, but Genesis makes it clear that the breath of life came from God. God created us as living beings through the gift of breath. This story is echoed at the end of the Gospel of John, when Jesus breathed into the apostles, saying, "Receive the Holy Spirit" (John 20:22). This is why we refer to the Holy Spirit as the "giver of life" in the Nicene Creed. Jesus Christ breathed into us a life like his own with the power of the Holy Spirit.

Breathing into an NES cartridge gave the game new life. Likewise, God breathes life into us through the Holy Spirit. We need to breathe to survive, but God sustains us with spiritual breath as well. He animates our lives with his breath at birth and in our new birth in baptism when we become Christian disciples and the children of God. Like an NES cartridge needing air to operate correctly, we need the breath of God and the Holy Spirit to operate the way that he intends us to live.

CHAPTER 40
ASCENSION OFF THE SCREEN

Early arcade games were limited to a single, unmoving screen of gameplay. In games like *Joust*, *Pac-Man*, and *Asteroids*, you could exit the screen on one side and then reenter on the other side. These games were called wraparounds because the sides of the screen wrapped around together.

Eventually, vertical-scrolling and side-scrolling video games became increasingly popular, especially with the rise of Nintendo's *Super Mario Bros.* As the character moved, the screen moved, keeping Mario or the other game characters in view.

Sega introduced an interesting concept in its side-scroller video game *Sonic the Hedgehog*. With its emphasis on speed, Sonic was so fast that he sometimes ran or catapulted off the screen. It would take a few moments, but the screen would eventually catch up to him.

We can imagine that the disciples felt a similar sense of loss when Jesus ascended into heaven. In video games we get used to seeing characters on screen. It feels unnatural not to see the characters we've become accustomed to seeing in the game. But with Jesus's final words, he ascended out of view of the disciples, and yet they stood staring in his direction, waiting for him to reappear.

Two angels appeared to the disciples at the ascension and said, "Men of Galilee, why do you stand looking up toward heaven? This Jesus, who has been taken up from you into heaven, will come in the same way as you saw him go into heaven" (Acts 1:11). Unlike Sonic, who eventually reenters the screen, or Pac-Man, who reappears on the opposite side of the screen after exiting, Jesus's body is not coming back—at least not yet.

Jesus Christ ascended into heaven and is now seated at the right hand of the Father. His body is not here. It is with God in heaven. We believe, however, he will return. He will come again, but we may have to wait a lot longer than the amount of time it takes Sonic to reappear again in our side-scrolling game of life.

CHAPTER 41
WITNESSES TO THE ENDS OF THE METAVERSE

Roblox is more than a video game—it is a platform for people to gather in a collection of unique gaming worlds. *Roblox* allows users to create their own games and experience the games that others have created. With customizable avatars and accessories, players can explore multiple genres of games. The platform empowers young people to cultivate creativity and play by creating worlds within the world of *Roblox*.

Roblox's rise in popularity came at a time when there was an increasing interest in virtual worlds. As people spend more time immersed in video game platforms like *Roblox*, *Fortnite*, MMORPGs (massively multiplayer online role-playing games), and others, they increasingly have interactions with people in what we might call a metaverse. Videos games, especially in a platform like *Roblox*, are no longer just games—they are places to meet and interact with other human beings, even if it is through a digital avatar.

In his parting words to the apostles before his ascension into heaven, Jesus said, "You will be my witnesses in

Jerusalem, in all Judea and Samaria, and to the ends of the earth" (Acts 1:8). Likewise, in Matthew's account of Jesus's parting words to his followers, he commissioned them to "go therefore and make disciples of all nations" (Matthew 28:19). For this reason Christians have shared the good news about Jesus Christ with everyone and anyone all throughout the world.

In *Roblox* and other gaming platforms, people live and meet in a virtual world. The metaverse should be seen as a new part of the "ends of the earth." Therefore, as Christians we enter these video gaming worlds as witnesses of Jesus Christ. We are not asked to force our beliefs on anyone, but we are called to live a life of joyfully loving of our neighbor. Living a Christlike life with the help of the Holy Spirit is essential. Later, when it becomes appropriate, we can answer questions and share the reasons why we have become Christ's followers.

Jesus's parting words are important. He ascended into heaven. His body is not on earth, and he has no avatar in any video gaming world. But he has us. We are Christ's body now. To put it in another way, we are Christ's *avatar* now, meeting new people and inviting them to hear the message that has compelled us to know, love, and serve the Lord.

PART THREE
THE CHURCH

CHAPTER 42
CHRIST'S GAME ENGINE

In order to streamline the process of creating video games, many developers create game engines as frameworks to allow other designers to work on their games. Once the game engine is created, it can be used like a template to create more levels and even other games. Shigeru Miyamoto and his team at Nintendo, for example, created an in-house engine for side-scrolling games *Excitebike* (1984) and then *Super Mario Bros.* (1985). The game engine allowed designers to create new levels with the same elements stored in the game engine.

Id Software used a similar approach in the creation of their *Wolfenstein 3D*, *Doom*, and *Quake* franchises. John Carmack created a game engine for each of these games that enabled his partner, John Romero, and other designers to create unique levels. It streamlined the development process and allowed them to maintain a small team when their company was first starting out.

While Epic Games is best known as the creator of the hit game *Fortnite: Battle Royale*, their primary source of revenue for many years was their game engine. When developing the video game *Unreal*, they also created a 3D computer graphics game engine called the Unreal Engine. Some of the most successful games of the time were created in Unreal Engine, including *PUBG*, *Final Fantasy VII Remake*, *Valorant*, and of course *Fortnite*. The engine was even used to create special effects in the hit Star Wars show *The Mandalorian*.

As Christians we also have a sort of game engine that has allowed us to carry on for thousands of years after Jesus died, rose, and ascended into heaven. We call this game engine the Church. Jesus appointed twelve apostles, like the twelve tribes of Israel, to lead his followers after he was gone. He gave them the power of the Holy Spirit and instilled in them the authority to lead his people.

With each new generation of Christians, a new generation of leaders also rises to take the place of others. The apostles appointed bishops to lead the Church and pass on what had been handed on to them. The Church did not need to be re-created again and again. Christianity's game engine had already been given to the Church by Jesus Christ. Each new generation of leaders only has to decide how to adapt and grow to a changing world by relying on the gift of the Holy Spirit.

CHAPTER 43
DISCIPLES CALLED TO DUTY

The *Call of Duty* video game franchise has been a breakout success, beginning with the first installment in 2003 and then a megahit with the 2007 release of *Call of Duty 4: Modern Warfare*. The series has collectively sold hundreds of millions of copies and broke the Guinness World Records for the best-selling first-person shooter game series. In the early games of the series, players control an infantry soldier during World War II and play as modern soldiers in later games.

Unlike earlier first-person shooter games like *Doom*, *Quake*, and *GoldenEye 007*, the *Call of Duty* series offered an important new feature. In most first-person shooters, players fight alone. They infiltrate levels, explore, and fight against bad guys all by themselves. In *Call of Duty*, however, players fight alongside other NPC (non-player character) soldiers to complete missions. In later editions, players can even control multiple members of a party. As the opening lines of the original *Call of Duty* montage say, "In the war that changed the world, victory was not achieved by one man but by the lives of many."

In a similar way, the Church is made of disciples called into duty not alone but in groups. Christ did not call a collection of independent heroes. He called disciples and sent them forth as a community to save the world.

Whenever he sent out his disciples to do his work, he sent them out in groups. After he appointed twelve disciples as his Twelve Apostles, he "began to send them out two by two and gave them authority over the unclean spirits" (Mark 6:7). Not just the Apostles, but he sent forth his other disciples in groups as well. "The Lord appointed seventy-two others and sent them on ahead of him in pairs to every town and place where he himself intended to go" (Luke 10:1).

As Christians we often place too much burden on ourselves to make a difference in the world. Serving as a disciple can be tiresome and overwhelming, but Jesus said that "my yoke is easy, and my burden is light" (Matthew 11:30). One reason for this is that the burden is always shared. "For where two or three are gathered in my name, I am there among them" (Matthew 18:20). The Lord is present among us. We are not alone. He is with us, but so are our fellow brothers and sisters in Christ.

Who are the fellow disciples called to duty by your side? Who is fighting with you to spread the good news and bring Jesus into the world? Be grateful for the people who share in this fellowship. Our victory is not achieved alone but along with the lives of many.

CHAPTER 44
LFM

You might come across the abbreviation LFM, meaning "looking for more," in chat boxes of video games. The phrase is especially popular in MMORPGs like *World of Warcraft* or *Final Fantasy XIV*. LFM could also mean "looking for member," as people search for additional party members to help complete a campaign or defeat a big boss.

Posting LFM in a chatroom is a great metaphor for the Church. The Church is always looking for new members as disciples, leaders, and brothers and sisters in Christ. The reason, however, is about more than recruiting new, passive believers. The Church is a group of people looking for members to come to know Jesus and then help make the world a better place. Just as a person in a video game might join a group to accomplish a task, new Christians get involved in the Church to do good work in the world.

Jesus Christ was LFM in the gospels. He appointed the Twelve Apostles, the seventy-two disciples, and more to go out and spread the message about the kingdom of God. "[He] sent them on ahead of him in pairs to every town and place where he himself intended to go" (Luke 10:1). Today, centuries later, we join with other disciples to continue this mission to go where Jesus intends us to go. We never go alone. We always go in groups of two or more to accomplish this mission.

CHAPTER 45
WATCHING ONE-PLAYER GAMES

One of my earliest memories of *Super Mario Bros.* is sitting around the TV at a neighbor's house with a group of kids watching one another play. Everyone had to take turns because there were too many of us. I remember my turns being short since I didn't have a Nintendo yet and I wasn't used to video games.

Watching a one-player game can get boring. Years later I celebrated my twelfth birthday party with a group of guys. I was 75 percent of the way through *The Legend of Zelda: A Link to the Past* on SNES, and the rental return was due back the next day. I made the guys watch me play during the party. Fun, right? I was a terrible host.

Life can feel like this too sometimes. We're not always the hero. Sometimes we are spectators of the lives of people around us. We have a choice. We can be bored and resentful that the spotlight isn't on us, or we can be kind and encouraging.

This comes about as easy as praying for the first time. Prayer requires humility. When we pray for others, we must humble ourselves and seek good for them. Prayer is a lot like watching a one-player game. We don't have to be passive observers. We can be active supporters. "Pray for one another" (James 5:16) as Saint James urged us to do.

Imagine if people watching a one-player game could actually influence the game itself? Imagine if their prayers helped the player win the game? The game sees the support, hears the prayer, and helps the player with power-ups.

Pray for the other players in your life. Give them some support. Ask the Designer to help them as they play the game of life.

CHAPTER 46
CALLED LIKE A CHARACTER IN AN RPG

Inspired by the rise in fantasy literature and tabletop role-playing games like *Dungeons & Dragons*, role-playing games (RPGs) have historically been one of the most popular genres in video games. Players wield swords and magic in games like *Final Fantasy*, *Dragon Quest*, *World of Warcraft*, *The Witcher*, and *The Elder Scrolls*. Some games also feature elements of science fiction with RPG mechanics, like *Fallout*, *Star Wars: Knights of the Old Republic*, and *Mass Effect*.

RPGs include the many interweaving story lines of a party of characters and non-player characters. The games are called "role-playing" because you take on the identity of a character within the story of the game. Each player in the game that you control has a unique story line with unique skills, weapons, and attacks during the game.

Cloud is the only character in *Final Fantasy VII* that can wield a broadsword, and Barret is the only character with a gun-arm. Many characters in these fantasy RPGs take on classic tropes of fighter, magic-wielding wizards, and healers. In every case, each character is unique, with special skills to offer.

Just as each character in an RPG is unique, so too is each one of us unique. We are all given by God a special set of skills, talents, and abilities that can be grown and developed through life, as if we were gaining experience points in an RPG. The more we try to be a kind of character that we are not, the more we fall short of our purpose.

God has given us these unique interests and abilities for a reason. Jesus's first disciples were fishermen. He didn't call them out of their lives to become scholars. "Follow me, and I will make you fishers of people" (Matthew 4:19), he told them. They continued to play the role God had given them, but as disciples.

Later Saint Paul wrote to the members of the church in Corinth about embracing the unique roles to play. He explained that each of us is given a variety of spiritual gifts from the one Spirit. He went on to describe the Church as the Body of Christ, with some of us playing the role of hands and others acting as feet, but none more important than others.

"Do all work powerful deeds? Do all possess gifts of healing?" (1 Corinthians 12:29–30). Just as a party within an RPG has fighters and healers, so too are you called to play a specific role within the Church. As you grow and discern God's spiritual gifts in your life, you start to see ways in which you are living out what God made you to be. Don't try to be a different character. Embrace your gifts and play the character God called you to be.

CHAPTER 47
DRAFTING OTHER DISCIPLES

Drafting or slipstreaming is a technique used in racing to overcome wind resistance. If a cyclist or race car rides behind another racer, then the overall drag of the wind can be reduced to save energy and pick up speed.

In the *Mario Kart* video game series, players can ride behind other racers to get a short speed boost. The boost is a quick but effective way to pick up speed. It is a good reminder that winning in *Mario Kart* requires an awareness of what the other racers are doing.

In the Christian life, it is important to draft other disciples. In other words, watch what other Christians are doing and follow in their footsteps. "Be imitators of me, as I am of Christ" (1 Corinthians 11:1), Saint Paul wrote to his fellow disciples. Some Christians engage in a formal discipleship relationship, but anyone eager to grow in holiness can watch and follow the model of another disciple. Watch how they pray. Listen to how they speak. See the way they interact with others.

Draft another disciple and you will get a little boost in your spiritual journey. It may be short and spontaneous, but eventually you learn from what others have done and integrate it into your own way of life. From there the habits and practices you have learned will be the inspiration for others to grow in holiness as well. Soon other Christians will be drafting as disciples behind you.

CHAPTER 48
NOOB NOW AND FOREVER

In video game lingo, a "noob" is someone so new to a game that they make common mistakes from inexperience. It can also be used as an insult for someone who has experience but is making mistakes like a beginner. No one wants to be a noob.

Yet Christianity is full of noobs. This was intentional. Jesus called his followers "disciples," which refers to someone who learns from another person. Not only were Jesus's followers called disciples, the depiction of these disciples in the gospels shows a collection of people that were constantly making mistakes. To put it plainly, the models for the rest of Christian history were a bunch of noobs.

The experts in Judea, on the other hand, were called Pharisees. They were scholars of the Law. They criticized Jesus and his disciples for their failure to follow the Mosaic law correctly. Then ultimately they sought to kill Jesus for the things he said and did that threatened their perfect image of the world.

What did Jesus's noobs do when Jesus was arrested? They abandoned him. They scattered in fear. Saint Peter even denied knowing his teacher Jesus Christ. Thankfully, their story did not end there. Jesus returned to his disciples and gave them his Spirit to help guide them.

Led by the Spirit, but remaining disciples, the Apostles went out responding to Jesus's call to "go . . . make disciples of all nations" (Matthew 28:19). Christians today are those disciples. We are always learning and never experts. To be called a noob in Christianity is no insult. A noob is what we are now and forever. We are willing to make mistakes, learn from them, and seek God's forgiveness as we get back up and try again. Be a noob for God, never trying to be perfect and always learning.

CHAPTER 49
DON'T BE A MOB

Mob (or MOB) is short for "mobile object" or "mobile entity" in video games. Mobs include NPCs (non-player characters), monsters, animals, and other entities that roam around a specific area. When mobs were first introduced in video games of the 1980s, it was revolutionary for an object to roam and wander with a specific purpose and regardless of the player's actions. Now mobs and NPCs are quite commonplace in open-world games and MMORPGs.

The use of the term *mob* is particularly popular within the video game *Minecraft*. Mobs include animals, hostile monsters, and villagers that naturally spawn in certain areas. These mobs can be attacked or hurt by the player or another mob, and some can attack back.

The mobs in *Minecraft* and other games just wander through the world. They stay mostly in one location and roam around without meaning or purpose. A player, on the other hand, has agency. They have a purpose and interact with the mobs on the way toward fulfilling that purpose.

Jesus calls us to a higher purpose. He calls us out of our ordinary life of survival and work to something more. Simon, Andrew, James, and John were ordinary fisherman doing ordinary jobs, then one day Jesus saw them. He called them, saying, "Follow me, and I will make you fishers of people" (Matthew 4:19). This would be like a *Minecraft* player transforming a villager from a mob into a player, leaving their programmed location to go out and find an adventure.

When Jesus called the fishermen to follow him, the Scriptures say that "immediately they left" (Matthew 4:20) their nets and boats and followed him. They would become Jesus's apostles for their willingness to leave behind the ordinary life for something extraordinary.

Don't be a mob. Don't be like a meaningless mobile object wandering a tiny section of the wide world. Heed the call of Christ to become something more.

CHAPTER 50
LEAD THE LEMMINGS

The video game *Lemmings* became popular in the 1990s on both the personal computer and video game systems like SNES and Sega. The premise of the game is based on the popular myth that the lemming, a type of rodent, was prone to herd behavior so strong that they would follow their fellow lemmings to their deaths. The goal of the *Lemmings* video game is to prevent as many lemmings from walking off a cliff as possible.

In the game, the lemmings drop down from the ceiling into a room and immediately start to walk in a line. They never stop following the lemming in front of them. The continuous walking behind the leader often leads to their death unless the player can set up a path for safe passage to the exit. Players intervene by assigning specific tasks, like digging or building stairs to avoid obstacles.

Jesus once looked with compassion on his people because they were like "sheep without a shepherd" (Matthew 9:36). To put it in another way, they were like lemmings without a leader. As human beings we also have a natural herd instinct. We are inclined to lead and follow one another.

The problem is we often follow the wrong people. We are like the lemmings who carelessly follow the other lemmings in front of us. There were a lot of bad leaders during Jesus's day. They were "blind guides of the blind," and Jesus warned "if one blind person guides another, both will fall into a pit" (Matthew 15:14).

Today we follow successful people of the world and unknowingly fall into a pit. We see the way someone lives and the things they have and follow them without any idea where their life is leading us. We seek the wrong goals in life, like success, attractiveness, greed, and glory.

God also calls certain people to be better leaders. He calls to himself disciples who will lead others to a different way of life. Like the lemmings who dig, build, and block other lemmings from falling into a pit, the Christian disciple prevents others from falling in life.

We all need someone to follow. Christians, in all their imperfections, walk in a way that leads to freedom. Pick the right people to follow. Jesus Christ is the way. Walk behind his disciples and find peace and joy in this life, then look behind and see others walking behind you. The follower is also a leader. Follow Jesus and you will find yourself leading others to him as well.

PART FOUR
THE ENEMIES

CHAPTER 51
WHO IS THE BOSS?

Video games, like movies, are known for their villains. To beat a game, you have to beat the boss. To get to the last level, you have to beat many mini-bosses along the way, each getting more difficult to defeat than the last.

Each video game has unique main characters with unique bosses. Mario must defeat Bowser. Link must defeat Ganon (or Ganondorf) in *The Legend of Zelda*. Sonic the Hedgehog must defeat Dr. Eggman. Snake must defeat Liquid Snake in *Metal Gear Solid*. In *Street Fighter* you must defeat M. Bison. In *Mortal Kombat* you must defeat Goro. The list goes on.

Bosses are unique within each game and present unique challenges. They often require players to use recently learned skills to defeat them in battle. Once you defeat a mini-boss, you work your way up toward another one until you defeat the final boss.

Beating bosses is like defeating sin and temptations in our lives. Each of us has unique temptations and sins that we struggle with. Just as bosses are different in different games, so too are the temptations different for different people.

Defeating a sin and temptation is like defeating a mini-boss. You continue to level up, and new temptations arise even more difficult than the others. Sometimes bosses and mini-bosses return. Mario must pass a new version of Bowser at every level. The player character in *Elden Ring* must repeatedly defeat recurring bosses taking new forms with new weapons.

What boss are you fighting against today? What sin and temptation are you trying to overcome? It is worth the time to examine your life and the bosses that repeatedly stand in your way. With the gift of grace like new weapons in a game, defeat the bosses and overcome your unique temptations.

CHAPTER 52
ARMED AGAINST DIABLO

When people think about the devil, they tend to picture in their minds an image of a red demon with horns, surrounded by fire. In other words, they tend to imagine characters like the monsters in the *Diablo* video game series. They are gruesome and scary, like the stuff of nightmares.

Make no mistake. The devil is real. Hell is real. Demons are real. But the truth is that we do not see them. We don't wield physical weapons to battle against them and send them back into some fire-filled dungeon.

Diablo is the Spanish word for "devil." It comes from the Greek word *diabolos*, which means literally to "throw across." Another way of translating the word might be "divide." It is the opposite of the word *symbolon*, which means "throw with" or "throw together."

Set aside the images of demons with horns and instead focus on just this one concept: the devil divides. He is the great divider. From his first appearance in Genesis to his final defeat in Revelation, his entire goal is to divide us from God and one another. In other words, he tempts us to sin and separates us from God and others.

Yet we still must defend ourselves. We may not arm ourselves with spells and swords as in *Diablo*. But Saint Paul reminds us to "put on the whole armor of God, so that you may be able to stand against the wiles of the devil, for our struggle is not against blood and flesh but against the . . . spiritual forces of evil in the heavenly places" (Ephesians 6:11–12). He goes on to describe the kind of armor we do need in defense against the devil (Ephesians 6:14–17):

- "Belt your waist with truth"
- "Put on the breastplate of righteousness"
- "Lace up your sandals in preparation for the gospel of peace"
- "Take the shield of faith"
- "Take the helmet of salvation"
- "Take the sword of the Spirit, which is the word of God"

With these spiritual weapons and armor, we defend against the devil, who seeks to divide us from each other and from God. While we may not fight against a physical or even ghostly demon, we must fight an inner battle against the devil. This is why we turn to the gospel in the Bible and defend ourselves against the great divider with faith in God. You know you are at war when you feel a division between you and another person or between you and God. Arm yourself against these temptations.

CHAPTER 53
FIRST-PERSON SINNERS

The first-person shooter (FPS) games have continually been among the most popular video game genres. FPS's began with *Wolfenstein 3D* (1992), followed by *Doom* (1993), and many others, including *Half-Life*, *GoldenEye 007*, *Halo*, *Call of Duty*, and *Overwatch*. In these games players take the first-person perspective of a fighter, armed with various weapons, but usually guns.

Jesus strictly forbade unprovoked violence in his teachings. "For all who take the sword will die by the sword" (Matthew 26:52), he warned his disciples. He also advised his disciples on responding to violence saying, "If anyone strikes you on the right cheek, turn the other also" (Matthew 5:39).

There are, however, numerous examples of violence in the Bible. In the Old Testament God protects and supports the Israelites as they defeat and defend against their enemies. Jesus overthrows this kind of violence by the way he willingly gives up his life and suffers and dies in innocence.

At the end of the Bible, there is one last example of violence in Revelation. A war is happening right now whether we see it or not. It is a war between heaven and hell, between angels and demons. There has been a long tradition of what some have referred to as "spiritual warfare" that Christians have taken up in opposition to Satan and evil spirits. Saint Michael the Archangel, and the other angels, defend and fight against these evil spirits.

We can take up this fight as well in our resistance to sin and temptation. It can feel like the relentless attack of monsters or bad guys in a first-person shooter game. They are coming for us, and we have to defend ourselves.

The best defense against sin and temptation is prayer. There are many forms of prayer, just as there are many forms of weapons in a first-person shooter game. As we get better at using certain weapons in video games, so too can we get better at practicing certain forms of prayer and meditation. Temptations will never end in this life—in fact, the more you grow in holiness, the stronger Satan will attack.

Once we recognize this battle within us, we can take up spiritual arms to defend ourselves. Remember to "put on the whole armor of God," Saint Paul wrote, "so that you may be able to stand against the while of the devil" (Ephesians 6:11). It is wise, therefore, to learn to pray and practice Christian meditation. These practices help to defend against temptation and enable us to grow closer to God.

CHAPTER 54
TECMO TEMPTATIONS

Tecmo Bowl (1987) is a classic arcade and Nintendo football video game. With simple graphics and basic gameplay, millions of people experienced an eight-bit version of football in a player-versus-player mode or against a computer. In later versions people even played with some of their favorite NFL teams and players.

Today's football games, like *John Madden Football*, offer a wide variety of plays in the playbook. As an early football video game, *Tecmo Bowl* only offered four plays. The offense selected one of the four plays, while the defense tried to predict what play would be picked. If the defense picked the same play as the offense, then defenders ran right over the offensive line, usually causing a sack or an interception. It was almost impossible for the offense to succeed when the defense predicted the right play.

In the spiritual life, temptation can be a lot like *Tecmo Bowl*. The devil knows our weaknesses. Sometimes those weaknesses lead us to give in to temptations. Like *Tecmo Bowl* we find ourselves failing when the devil predicts our weakness.

Thankfully, we get another try. We turn to Jesus, asking for forgiveness, and pick another play to attempt a first down or touchdown. There is always the risk of a great temptation, but we keep fighting anyway because we know that we can succeed in overcoming those spiritual weaknesses.

The good thing to know is that we all play defense too. We know the predictable plays that the devil will use against us. We know the repeated lies we tell ourselves when facing temptation. We can see a temptation coming and prepare ourselves to fight it ahead of time.

Think about temptation to sin as Tecmo Temptations. Sometimes we can predict when they are coming and prepare to resist. Sometimes we face overwhelming attacks and fail. But we get back up and try again. Always be prepared for what's next.

CHAPTER 55
SOUL CRUSHING

The popularity of tile-matching video games began in the 1980s with *Tetris* and continued to find new audiences with new iterations like *Bejeweled* in the early 2000s and the perennial hit *Candy Crush* in 2013. The *Candy Crush Saga* began on Facebook but successfully transferred its success into the mobile app platforms.

Like other tile-matching video games, players must connect identical candies in *Candy Crush* to remove them from the screen. The simplicity of the game coupled with the flashing rewards and congratulatory sounds make it—for lack of a better word—addicting. Players get a small dopamine hit every time they clear a row, and sometimes an avalanche of rewards occur from one quick swipe of the finger on the screen. The short-term rewards keep players engaged and attempting to beat higher levels for long periods of time. People often don't realize how long they are playing during one sitting.

Christians categorize sins into two groups. There is mortal sin, which separates us from God. A mortal sin would be something like intentional murder or cursing God's name.

But Christians also identify the guilt of committing smaller sins, called venial sins, that weaken our connection to God and others. Candy is not evil, but being unable to control ourselves and eating too much candy shows our weakness. A little lie about ourselves to friends or family may seem harmless, but we weaken our relationship with them by spreading the falsehood.

The rewards in *Candy Crush* are a lot like the experience of venial sins. We pursue the short-term pleasure of matching candies to get a reward. The game seems harmless. It's fun to win. The more we win, however, the more we want to win again. The quick pleasures become a constant, almost uncontrollable pursuit of more any time we have a quick second to play.

When playing a game like *Candy Crush*, players sometimes feel a numbness in realizing how long they have played. This is the feeling the author of Ecclesiastes described when he wrote "Vanity of vanities! All is vanity" (Ecclesiastes 1:2) and "all the deeds that are done under the sun, and see, all is vanity and a chasing after wind" (Ecclesiastes 1:14). *Vanity* in this sense is the feeling of worthlessness or futility and pointlessness in life. Saint Paul wrote something similar when he explained that one who "lives for pleasure is dead even while she lives" (1 Timothy 5:6).

Be on the lookout for the soul-crushing feeling of vanity and chasing after the wind. What pursuit of short-term pleasures is causing this feeling of pointlessness? What felt good but is slowly pulling you away from God and giving you that sense of meaninglessness? It is a sign to turn away from the short-term rewards and seek the long-term joy of focusing on God instead.

CHAPTER 56
SHOOT 'EM UP

The hit arcade game *Space Invaders* (1978) ushered in an entire genre of video games. *Asteroids*, *Centipede*, *Galaga*, and many more games created the shoot-'em-up style of gaming. Shoot 'em ups were exactly as they sound. Players on the ground or in spaceships shoot at almost endless number of enemies, dodge their attacks, and protect themselves or the bottom of the screen.

To win a shoot-'em-up game is to eliminate the enemies and create an empty sky. Remove the enemies and restore peace. We do something similar in the Christian life.

A part of our task as Christians is to eliminate sinful habits and temptations from our lives. Saint Paul wrote, "Put to death, therefore, whatever in you is earthly: sexual immorality, impurity, passion, evil desire, and greed (which is idolatry). . . . But now you must get rid of all such things: anger, wrath, malice, slander, and abusive language from your mouth" (Colossians 3:5, 8).

Thankfully, we are not alone. Jesus came to help us eliminate these temptations and offer forgiveness of sins. "You know that he was revealed to take away sins, and in him there is no sin" (1 John 3:5). In Jesus we find the peace of an empty sky after putting to death the sin-like space invaders.

While we may not be able to overcome our greatest temptations without God's help, we can take the time to identify which temptations we are struggling with the most. Taking time to examine our conscience and discovering where bad habits have entered our lives is very important. Like scanning the sky for asteroids, missiles, or alien spaceships, scan through your thoughts and actions and find what needs to be eliminated. Then bring those temptations to the Lord for mercy and help to remove them from your life in the future.

CHAPTER 57
DON'T FINISH HIM

When *Mortal Kombat* debuted in 1992, it was one of the bloodiest, most violent video games in history. It was also one of the most popular games in the world. An entire franchise of games, movies, TV shows, and toys followed its breakout success.

One of the memorable features of the original fighting game was the fatality move. After defeating your opponent, an ominous voice would announce "FINISH HIM." With a certain sequence of buttons, a player could kill the opponent in an especially gruesome and merciless way.

We can hear a similar voice in our heads sometimes. In movies and cartoons it is often characterized by a little devil on the shoulder, speaking temptations into someone's ear. Indeed, that voice of temptation comes from outside of us. It is the voice of Satan, the devil who constantly seeks to turn us toward sin and away from God.

We may not hear an actual voice speaking these temptations with instructions to do evil. The devil tempts us with a wordless desire to not only win but destroy anyone in the way of what we want. Performing a finishing move in *Mortal Kombat* is unnecessary. The fight is over. You already won, but the fatality move provides an entertaining and gruesome achievement on top of the victory.

There are so many chances in our lives to prove we are better than others, but Jesus taught another way. He told his disciples to love their enemies. He told them to be perfect, as their Father in heaven is perfect. He said to be merciful, as their Father is merciful.

The life of a Christian is having the strength to resist the voice saying "FINISH HIM" and instead show mercy. Christians compete well, but they do so with respect for others and humility in victory. Just because you know you are better doesn't mean you have to show it.

CHAPTER 58
POWER-UPS OF GRACE

Video games are classically known for their power-ups. What would Mario be without Super Mushrooms, Fire Flowers, and Super Stars? Sonic finds shields and Power Sneakers along his journeys. Pac-Man eats Power Pellets, and many heroes find power-ups in treasure chests during their RPG adventures.

There is a theological lesson behind power-ups in video games. Power-ups come from the outside, not the inside. We cannot conjure up special abilities from within. The power-ups are gifts we find along the way, outside of ourselves.

Power-ups are a helpful metaphor for what Christians call *grace*. Grace is a gift of God's help and holiness. Grace helps us overcome challenges in our lives. Grace instills in us charisms that make us who we are. Grace sanctifies us and makes us holy so that we may live like Jesus Christ.

The word *grace* means "favor" or "gift." Just like a power-up in a video game, grace is a gift to be discovered outside of ourselves. We cannot conjure up grace through spiritual feelings or hard work. We receive grace as a gift through faith and openness to the Holy Spirit.

We receive grace from the Holy Spirit in many ways, but primarily through the sacraments, prayer, penance, and charity. In these ways we are open to the power-ups God is giving to us.

How do we know grace exists? We don't necessarily feel more powerful when we receive actual graces from God. We don't grow in size or have the ability to throw fireballs. We do, however, change. As Jesus said, "You will know them by their fruits" (Matthew 7:20). Just as you see the fruits of the power-ups (fireballs, shields, etc.), you see the work of grace in the lives of people who bear good fruit.

What does grace actually do for us? What is happening within us that goes unseen? Let's turn specifically to Pac-Man to extend this analogy a little further in the role of grace against sin.

CHAPTER 59
PAC-MAN PELLETS OF GRACE

Pac-Man took the world by storm in the 1980s. In each level of the game, players guide Pac-Man through a maze to eat all the yellow dots and avoid four colored ghosts (Blinky, Inky, Pinky, and Clyde). Once all the yellow dots are consumed, the level is completed.

The ghosts are always chasing Pac-Man. They are never satisfied and never relent. Even after they are defeated, they continue to come back again.

The only way to defeat the ghosts is to escape them or eat one of the four Power Pellets that enable Pac-Man to chase the ghosts for a short amount of time. If he catches them, they will return to the center of the maze until the impact of the Power Pellets wears off.

Like all power-ups, the power comes from the outside. Pac-Man cannot power up himself without eating the Power Pellets. Likewise, Christians cannot access God's gift of grace without faith and openness to the Holy Spirit.

The ghosts in the Pac-Man game series are a lot like sin and Satan. Sin and temptation are relentless. Sin is never satisfied. Even after a temptation to sin is defeated, it comes back again, attacking us in new ways. When sin finally catches up with us, it takes our lives, just like the ghosts in the game.

We cannot defeat sin on our own, just as Pac-Man cannot defeat the ghosts without the Power Pellets. When we are struggling with any kind of bad habit or temptation, we need to turn outward, not inward. First we need to recognize where sin is and avoid it. But we cannot run forever, and we cannot defeat Satan on our own. When we turn to God for his help, then the Lord's grace enables us to stand strong. Like the Power Pellets in Pac-Man, grace is a gift from God to help us turn away from sin and be transformed.

Sin continues its pursuit. The devil is always at work. We must continually turn away from sin, like Pac-Man running from the ghosts. We go out in search of the grace again to overcome sin and temptation and become transformed into the person God intends us to be.

CHAPTER 60
ROLL THE GOLDEN MEAN

In ancient Greek philosophy, the "golden mean" is the middle of two extremes of either too much or too little. The philosopher Aristotle emphasized the golden mean in his writings about morality. The goal of human striving is to practice virtue, which is a behavior that shows a balance between two extremes. We call these extremes vices, and we should avoid them by focusing on a balance instead.

The traditional seven deadly sins are inspired in part by the philosophical tradition of virtues versus vices. The deadly sins of pride, lust, gluttony, greed, wrath, envy, and sloth express extreme and excessive desires. The virtues of prudence, justice, temperance, and fortitude express a balance (the golden mean) compared to the extremes of the seven vices.

Pursuing virtue and the golden mean is a lot like playing the classic arcade game *Golden Tee Golf*. Unlike many other arcade games, *Golden Tee* is played by rolling a ball rather than a joystick or directional pad. Players roll the ball (called the trackball) to control the distance and direction of a golfer's swing. Spin the ball too hard and the golfer on the screen will hit the ball too far and out of control. Spin the ball too gently and the player will barely tap the ball.

Look at your own life, including your actions and desires. Are you taking actions that show an excess desire for too much of something? Do you want too much money, too many possessions, too much food, or too much attraction to another person? Does it feel like you are trying too hard, like spinning a trackball too aggressively? Or are you not putting in enough effort, like barely tapping the trackball in *Golden Tee*? Whenever you feel yourself seeking too much or not desiring enough, you may find you need to seek the grace to find the golden mean. There you will find a virtuous and well-balanced life without being knocked out of control.

As Christians the key to seeking balance is to focus on the Lord. This is like focusing on the hole in *Golden Tee*. "Take delight in the LORD, and he will give you the desires of your heart" (Psalm 37:4). Or put in another way, "Be still before the LORD" (Psalm 37:7). "Be still, and know that I am God!" (Psalm 46:10). To place our desire and goal on anyone or anything else is spinning the trackball away from the goal. Focus on the Lord. Put God as your goal, and you will find peace and joy in life.

CHAPTER 61
GRAND PRIDE

C. S. Lewis called pride the father of all sins. Pride includes the belief that we are better than someone else and the actions that stem from the superiority. Pride is the opposite of humility. It was also called *hubris* in ancient Greece, referring to pride that leads to a fall. Aristotle described it as the shame we place on someone for our own gratification, not even to achieve personal gain but just to make others feel bad.

Pride runs rampant in the *Grand Theft Auto* series. The goal of the game is to rise in the ranks of the mafia by stealing cars and killing people while avoiding the police. In the original version of the game, before 3D graphics, it was easy to lose control of a car and run over or shoot innocent people. The game allows you to rip drivers out of their cars and speed away without remorse.

Sins of murder and theft are the basis of the game, but above these and other immoral acts in the game, we can point to the deadly sin of pride. *GTA* was one of the early open-world games. During the many games in the series, you can drive anywhere you choose to complete missions to advance the story line.

An open world invites the sin of pride to have free rein. You can go anywhere and do anything as long as you don't get caught. In time you become numb to the stealing and murder because of a sense of superiority. You are the player, and they are standing in the way of your victory.

Be warned. "Pride goes before destruction and a haughty spirit before a fall" (Proverbs 16:18). Instead, we should seek humility in life. "When pride comes, then comes disgrace, but wisdom is with the humble" (Proverbs 11:2). Follow your pride in the *GTA* series, and destruction follows. While you might rise in the ranks, the lives of unknown numbers of NPC people are destroyed.

In real life these crimes are unacceptable and lead to imprisonment. Pride, however, still runs rampant in our everyday lives. Do not think of yourself and your goals and needs as more important than others. In fact, the way of Christ is to put others before yourself and to humbly help those around you. "Just as I have loved you, you also should love one another" (John 13:34), Jesus said to his disciples. He did not take the lives of others but put the lives of others before his own and gave up his life for them. That is the sign of true humility and true Christian love.

CHAPTER 62
GREEDY RINGS

Sonic the Hedgehog races across the screen collecting golden rings along the way. As he runs, you can hear the ching-ching-ching of new rings being collected. The only problem is that sometimes he accidentally runs into enemies or spikes that cause him to lose all of those rings. Get hit again without any rings and Sonic dies.

Greed is one of the seven deadly sins. The sin of greed isn't contained in the money itself (or, in this case, golden rings). The sin is the desire for more money without any limit. Greed grows forever. When we know what we need, then greed goes away. When we can be happy with enough, then we resist the temptation of greed.

Taking damage in a *Sonic the Hedgehog* game gives us a good lesson. No matter how many rings you collect, one hit and they all go flying. Everything you hold on to for yourself eventually goes away. Jesus warned his disciples about this. "Do not store up for yourselves treasures on earth, where moth and rust consume and where thieves break in and steal, but store up for yourselves treasures in heaven . . . For where your treasure is, there your heart will be also" (Matthew 6:19–21).

Sonic only needs a few rings to avoid death. There are more than one hundred rings at every level but the Final Zone in the games. The reward of earning more rings drives the desire for more, but the fear of pain and death is also a motivator. Greed can be built upon a foundation of fear and worry. We worry we won't have enough and end up taking more than we need.

But we must be careful. "Which of you by worrying can add a single hour to your span of life?" (Matthew 6:27). Money and possessions never satisfy the fear. The worry about not having enough turns into a worry about losing what we have. But "one's life does not consist in the abundance of possessions" (Luke 12:15). Instead, enjoy the gifts we are given. Be grateful to God for what we have. Trust that he will take care of you. "So do not worry about tomorrow, for tomorrow will bring worries of its own. Today's trouble is enough for today" (Matthew 6:34).

CHAPTER 63
SLOTH OR JOUST

In the popular arcade game *Joust* (1982), players control a knight with a lance mounted on a large bird. The goal is to fly up into the air and defeat either enemy knights riding on buzzards or an opposing knight playing as Player 2.

The highest knight wins in *Joust*. The game functions a lot like *Flappy Bird* and the many similar video games that it inspired. The only way to fly up is to tap a button repeatedly—otherwise your knight floats to the ground or the platforms scattered around the screen. Fly to the end of the screen to the right and you appear at the same height on the left side of the screen.

The spiritual life can often feel like the game of *Joust*. Sloth is one of the seven deadly sins. Sloth sounds like spiritual laziness, and sometimes that is the way the sin is expressed. You know what you should do to grow in holiness and goodness, but you don't want to put in the work. It is like not pressing the button in *Joust* to fly up into the sky.

Sloth has a deeper dimension though, best expressed by the original Greek word for the sin of sloth: *acedia*. Acedia means "negligence" or "lack of care" in Greek. In *Joust* laziness would be not pressing the button fast enough, never elevating higher than the opponent and always soaring across the screen at low levels. But the source of the sin is lack of care about the spiritual life. It would be a player seeing the knight falter and deciding to just run across the ground instead of putting in the effort to defeat the opponents. There are just too many buzzards to defeat, so doing nothing seems like the better choice. You just don't care enough to try.

How do you overcome sloth/acedia? The closer you are to heaven, just like in a game of *Joust*, the more you grow in holiness. While it might not be fun or feel emotionally fulfilling, sometimes you must put in the work anyway. You must keep showing up in prayer, spiritual reading, and going to church during the dark or boring times. Yes, it takes effort, just like it takes effort to elevate the knight in *Joust*. Just keep flapping your spiritual wings and eventually you find yourself growing closer to God and experiencing the rewards of eternal life.

CHAPTER 64
MASSIVE MULTIPLAYER ENVY

Envy is the excessive desire for what other people have. There are two types of envy. We can envy someone's possessions, money, and status, or we can envy their characteristics, talents, or skills. To put it in terms of the Ten Commandments, we covet what other people have.

As the speed and use of the Internet grew in the late 1990s, the opportunity for a new kind of video game developed —MMORPG (massively multiplayer online role-playing game). While traditional RPGs are populated with NPCs, a MMORPG is made up of a large number of actual player characters. These games have become very popular among people who have put in countless hours in developing their characters. *World of Warcraft*, *EverQuest*, *RuneScape*, and *The Elder Scrolls Online* are among the most popular MMORPGs.

In these games players can develop their character's ability scores and gather items to increase their status and fighting ability. Along with these goals, however, comes the temptation of envy. It is easy to compare your character to the much more powerful characters in the world.

Players can easily become obsessed with increasing certain skills or obtaining certain items.

This is exactly how envy works in the real world. We see what others have and want it for ourselves. This desire for what others have leads to other sins of lying, cheating, or stealing in order to obtain what we want. "For where there is envy and selfish ambition, there will also be disorder and wickedness of every kind" (James 3:16). By avoiding envy in the first place, we can prevent these other sins as well.

As Christians we practice prayers of gratitude and blessing. When we are grateful for what we have and reliant upon God for the gifts he has given to us, we weaken envy in our hearts. Likewise, to bless the gifts of this world is to offer them up to God rather than hold on to them for ourselves. Everything is a gift. Nothing is ours to keep. Therefore, give thanks to God for what we have been given.

CHAPTER 65
ANGRY BIRDS AWAY

Since its release in 2009, the mobile game *Angry Birds* has been downloaded billions (yes, billions!) of times. In the game players launch a collection of ball-like birds with a slingshot to attack pig-like enemies. Once all of the pigs are toppled, players advance to the next level.

At each level those birds start out with scowl and stay angry until the level is complete. But then another level begins, and the birds are angry again. Players continue to advance to another level and another and another.

There were hundreds of levels in the original version of *Angry Birds*, and the creators added new chapters of the game during the first three years of the game's existence. *Angry Birds 2* has thousands of levels to master, and there have been dozens of other sequels and spin-off games.

Jesus warned against endless anger. "If you are angry with a brother or sister, you will be liable to judgment" (Matthew 5:22). Instead, Jesus and his disciples spread the message of forgiveness. He instructed us to pray "forgive us our debts, as we also have forgiven our debtors"

(Matthew 6:12). Saint Paul wrote to the Ephesians, "Put away from you all bitterness and wrath and anger . . . forgiving one another, as God in Christ has forgiven you" (Ephesians 4:31–32).

Anger is never satisfied. Like yet another level of *Angry Birds*, wrath continues to control us. Wrath is one of the seven deadly sins. The only solution is forgiveness. That doesn't make avoiding anger easy. All of us will become angry at one time or another. Even Jesus became angry from time to time (Mark 3:5).

Forgiveness is the key to making anger go away. Release its hold and let go of the bitterness that is holding you back.

CHAPTER 66

MR. GLUTTONY

In the classic arcade game *BurgerTime* (1982), players control a chef named Peter Pepper as he attempts to create hamburgers (bun, burger, lettuce, tomato, and another bun) while avoiding enemy foods. The game shares a design similar to *Donkey Kong*, as the player must navigate up and down ladders and across platforms. When the chef walks across an ingredient, it falls down. Once all the ingredients stack up at the bottom in the correct order, the burgers can be served.

Imagine this game as a metaphor for the deadly sin of gluttony. Gluttony describes the excessive desire to consume more food than necessary. Temperance is the corresponding virtue, which encourages a tamed desire to eat and enjoy food without overindulging.

The enemies in the game are Mr. Hot Dog, Mr. Pickle, and Mr. Egg. It is important to remember that gluttony is not sinful because of the foods but because of the excessive desire for food. In the game, the chef builds hamburgers and avoids adding the other foods, like hot dogs, pickles, and eggs. Hot dogs, pickles, and eggs are not sinful foods.

They are not evil in themselves. Foods are good and gifts from God, but we should avoid the temptation to eat more than necessary.

We have many warnings about this in the Bible. Hunger caused one of the earliest sins in the book of Exodus. "They tested God in their heart by demanding the food they craved" (Psalm 78:18). Christians, too, must beware of these temptations so that we do not become like those whose "god is the belly; and their glory is in their shame; their minds are set on earthly things" because "our citizenship is in heaven" (Philippians 3:19–20). "Instead," Saint Paul wrote, "put on the Lord Jesus Christ, and make no provision for the flesh, to gratify its desires" (Romans 13:14). Give up the desire for more and focus on temperance without overindulging.

CHAPTER 67
LUST FOR LARA CROFT

There have been many strong female heroines throughout video game history. The main character of *Metroid*, Samus Aran, shocked the male-dominated gaming world of the 1980s when she removed her helmet at the end of the game to reveal she was a woman. Fighting games have also had their tough female characters in *Street Fighter II* with Chun-Li and in *Mortal Kombat* with Sonya Blade, among others. These women are all beautiful and powerful heroines.

But at the top of many of the lists of best female video game characters ranks Lara Croft, archaeologist and adventurer in the *Tomb Raider* video game series. Croft made a splash in the mostly still male-dominated video game industry of the 1990s. By that time the quality of video game graphics on the PlayStation had become advanced enough for the creators of *Tomb Raider* to make a highly attractive humanlike main character.

Despite the series's critical and commercial success, naysayers jumped at the chance to attack the video game industry for its depiction of Lara Croft. With her short shorts and curvy physique, she became one of the first cultural sex icons in the gaming world. The reaction reveals a fear of the seventh deadly sin of lust.

Lust describes an attraction for someone that becomes so great we desire to use them for our personal pleasure. Beauty is good. Our physical attraction to that beauty is good, but when it goes too far into a personal desire to objectify and use someone for ourselves, then it becomes the deadly sin of lust.

There are two ways to protect ourselves against the sin of lust. First, we may just need to look away because even looking with lust is a sin in itself. Jesus said, "Everyone who looks at a woman with lust has already committed adultery with her in his heart" (Matthew 5:28). Jesus puts it even more bluntly: "If your right eye causes you to sin, tear it out and throw it away" (Matthew 5:29). While we may not take these words literally, we can acknowledge that sometimes we need to look away.

But the best way to be free from lust is to live by the Holy Spirit instead of the flesh. Remember that Christ gave the Holy Spirit to his disciples to write the law on our hearts (Jeremiah 31:33). As Saint Paul wrote, "Live by the Spirit, I say, and do not gratify the desires of the flesh" (Galatians 5:16). Do this and we will experience the fruit of the Spirit: "love, joy, peace, patience, kindness, generosity, faithfulness, gentleness, and self-control" (Galatians 5:22–23).

If gamers find themselves overly attracted to people like Lara Croft in games or the real world, then these two steps may be needed. Avoid the temptation by looking away, and then turn to the Spirit for help in seeking to experience the fruits of love, joy, peace, and self-control instead.

PART FIVE
GAMEPLAY GUIDE

CHAPTER 68
SIDE-SCROLLING SPIRITUALITY

In a side-scrolling video game, the screen follows the game's character from a side angle moving to the right and sometimes back to the left. *Super Mario Bros.* and *Sonic the Hedgehog* are the most popular early side scrollers. The classic beat-'em-up games like *Kung-Fu Master*, *Double Dragon*, *Battletoads*, and the original arcade game for *The Simpsons* also use a side-scrolling format.

It is helpful to think about life, especially the spiritual life, as a side-scrolling video game. In a side-scrolling game, you can only focus on the challenges right in front of you. In some of these games, like *Super Mario Bros.*, you cannot go backward. You cannot undo what you have done. In real life guilt about the past can lead to shame today, but we have to press on. As Christians we turn to God, seek his mercy, and with his grace move forward in life.

A side-scrolling video game also prevents us from thinking too far ahead. Many of the beat-'em-up side scrollers express this best, often pausing the screen's movement until all the enemies of a certain area are defeated. We have a tendency to worry about the future, which leads to anxiety today. But Jesus said to his disciples, "So do not worry about tomorrow, for tomorrow will bring worries of its own. Today's trouble is enough for today" (Matthew 6:34).

Focus on today and this moment. Don't let the mistakes of the past prevent you from dealing with the challenges today. God gives you his mercy. Don't let worry about the unpredictable future freeze your actions today. Place your trust in God with hope for the future. You will find more joy and peace as you focus on the present moment.

CHAPTER 69
REPENT AND RESET

Early video game consoles, including the Nintendo, Sega Genesis, and even the original PlayStation had a Reset button. Rather than turn the power off and on again, players could press the Reset button to reboot a game. This was sometimes needed when a game froze or whenever a player was stuck and wanted to start a game again.

The ability to push Reset on life is one of the defining characteristics of Christianity. There is no amount of mistakes that prohibit us from starting over with God. He is always willing to provide mercy and forgiveness if we are willing to change.

John the Baptist, Jesus, and the apostles all preach a message of repentance in the New Testament. "Repent and be baptized" (Acts 2:38), Peter preached in his early ministry. The Gospel of Mark opens with a description of John the Baptist in the wilderness "proclaiming a baptism of repentance for the forgiveness of sins" (Mark 1:4). People joined John in the wilderness, confessing their sins and seeking baptism. Jesus likewise preached this message with his opening words in the Gospel of Mark, saying,

"The time is fulfilled, and the kingdom of God has come near; repent, and believe in the good news" (Mark 1:15).

The Reset button is always available to us. As John and Peter said, baptism is one way for us to repent. Through baptism we die to ourselves and our sin and rise again with Jesus as a new creation. It is just like that Reset button. "Do you not know that all of us who were baptized into Christ Jesus were baptized into his death?" (Romans 6:3).

Thankfully, the Reset button is more than a onetime thing. Although we are baptized once, we can repeatedly turn to Jesus Christ, seeking repentance and a reset on life. "If we confess our sins, he who is faithful and just will forgive us our sins and cleanse us from all unrighteousness" (1 John 1:9). Through this confession of our sins, God grants us forgiveness. Like the prodigal son returned from a life of sinfulness, God comes running to us, welcoming us back in love to live a new life. We were lost and then found. We were dead but have come back to life. We were like the lost sheep whom the shepherd went out to find and bring home again. "There will be more joy in heaven over one sinner who repents than over ninety-nine righteous persons who need no repentance" (Luke 15:7).

No matter how far down a dark path you have gone, you can always press Reset. God is there, ready and willing to give you the chance to start over. Keep playing the game. Repent and get a reset on life.

CHAPTER 10
PUSH PAUSE

In the gospels Jesus often went off to a quiet place to pray. Even the Son of God needed a few moments to pause and collect himself before the day began.

One of the greatest inventions in video game history is the Pause button. Real life often requires us to take a break from a game. Click Pause and come back later to pick up where you left off.

We all need a divine Pause button in life sometimes. As it reads in the Psalms: "Be still, and know that I am God!" (Psalm 46:10). Or to put this in video game terms, "Click Pause, and know that I am God!"

We often think of prayer as a conversation with God. We feel compelled to talk all the time or, some would say, to listen as well. But prayer can be simple time spent with God without any words at all. Silence is so scarce these days. We need to experience silence in our lives.

The highest form of prayer is called contemplation. This form of Christian meditation is not intense focus on holy words or images. Contemplation, as Saint Teresa of Avila said, "means taking time frequently to be alone with him who we know loves us."[1]

Push Pause. Be still. The game of life will be waiting for you when you return. Take some time to be silent, then click the Pause button to begin again.

CHAPTER 71
MEEK LIKE MAC

The main character in the 1980s NES game *Mike Tyson's Punch-Out!!* is a young boxer named Little Mac. Mac is small with no special fighting abilities or knockout punches. He has a left and right jab, left and right body blows, and an uppercut that he can use after earning a star.

Mac faces a series of eccentric characters with powerful punches and special moves. After winning matches against Glass Joe, Piston Hurricane, Bald Bull, Mr. Sandman, Soda Popinksi, and more, Little Mac faces the final boss, Mike Tyson himself, in "The Dream Fight." (Later, Tyson was replaced by a character named Mr. Dream after Mike Tyson's license in the franchise expired.)

How does Little Mac succeed against such powerful opponents? In the Sermon on the Mount Jesus taught something shocking to his disciples. "Blessed are the meek, for they will inherit the earth" (Matthew 5:5). The word *meek* means "quiet," "gentle," and "mild." While all of the opponents in *Punch-Out!!* brag and use their powerful special moves, meek Little Mac patiently punches and dodges attacks on his way to victory.

In many ways Little Mac is a model for holiness. Being meek isn't weak. Christians rely on God for strength. Through patient perseverance a Christian is blessed by God to overcome challenges and find happiness.

As Saint Paul wrote to the Corinthians, "On my own behalf I will not boast, except of my weaknesses . . . for whenever I am weak, then I am strong" (2 Corinthians 12:5, 10). God gives strength within our weaknesses. "I can do all things through [Christ] who strengthens me" (Philippians 4:13).

It is unnatural to seek to be meek and humble. Instead, we would rather be praised for our victories. We would rather show of our powerful gifts (special moves) and take credit for our success. Instead, the Christian finds strength in weakness because God blesses the meek, just like Little Mac.

CHAPTER 72
AVATAR SKINS AND ACCESSORIES

In video games like *Roblox*, *Fortnite*, *Apex Legends*, and others, players can purchase skins and accessories for their avatars. An avatar is how a player's character appears in the game world. Gamers can obtain skins to reveal their personality and show off their good looks. It is a way for people to look impressive and admirable or even intimidating. Most of all, it's just fun for people to express their personalities in creative ways to stand out from the crowd.

As fun as this may be, Christians will recognize the dangerous path for those who focus too much on outward appearance. "Why do you worry about clothing?" (Matthew 6:28), Jesus asked his disciples. He reminded them to "seek first the kingdom of God and his righteousness" (Matthew 6:33) rather than worry about food and clothing. "Is not life more than food and the body more than clothing?" (Matthew 6:25).

We all want to express ourselves by the clothing we wear in the real world and as avatars in video games. It is important for us to be unique and confident in ourselves. But when we place our confidence in the outward appearance that we create for ourselves, then we worry more about what people think of us than who we really are.

Instead, focus on your heart. No avatar can express this in the skins they wear. "Do not adorn yourselves outwardly . . . rather, let your adornment be the inner self with the lasting beauty of a gentle and quiet spirit, which is very precious in God's sight" (1 Peter 3:3–4). More important than any appearance you might create in a video game is the way that you interact with the people behind the avatars and accessories you meet in the game worlds. Be yourself not just outwardly but in the way that you seek selflessness in the sight of others.

CHAPTER 13
BUILD VIRTUE LIKE TETRIS

Tetris is an iconic puzzle video game that took the world by storm in the 1980s. Made popular by the handheld Nintendo Game Boy edition, *Tetris* has since expanded to more than sixty-five platforms and reached the lives of millions of people.

The goal of *Tetris* is to rotate and align a collection of falling shapes called "tetrominoes" to form lines that disappear when completed. The more lines you complete at once, the more points you score. Completing four lines at once with the I-shaped tetromino is called a "tetris" and scores the most points. As you score more points and advance through levels, the pieces fall faster and faster, increasing the challenge of the game.

In the Christian life, a virtue is a habit that leads us to choose and do good. The human virtues like prudence, fortitude, justice, and temperance help us to practice the Golden Rule: "In everything do to others as you would have them do to you" (Matthew 7:12). The theological virtues of faith, hope, and love have God as the ultimate good goal and align our thoughts and actions completely on him.

Tetris became so popular that game players started to see Tetris patterns in their thoughts and sleep. This phenomenon became known as the Tetris Effect. Tetris became a part of how major players thought and saw the world.

Developing virtue tends to operate in the same way. God has given us a conscience. We know right from wrong. We develop virtues to practice right actions and good thoughts. The more we practice the virtues in small ways, the more we can apply them to difficult situations. They become a part of who we are. Just like completing lines in *Tetris* in creative and quick ways, we come up with new ways to live out the virtues.

Temperance, for example, is mastery over physical temptations. Like all virtues, it grows in strength through practice. By resisting the temptation to eat candy, for example, we grow our virtuous resistance to the greater physical temptations, like lust. We build virtue one act of resistance at a time, just like we complete one line of *Tetris* at a time.

As we advance through life and develop more virtues, greater difficulties seem to arise. The spiritual and moral life doesn't necessarily get easier, but we get stronger in our desire to do good. Just as a *Tetris* player acclimates to a faster-falling tetromino, we adapt our application of the virtues to seek and do good in our daily lives. Instead of the Tetris Effect, always seeing tetrominoes in our thoughts, we will experience a Virtue Effect, always seeing ways to act selflessly toward others.

CHAPTER 74
GATHER RESOURCES

Real-time strategy games became popular in the late 1990s beginning with the original *Warcraft*, *Warcraft II*, and then the breakout hits *StarCraft* and *StarCraft II*. The genre is called real-time strategy because players compete against the computer or other players in real time. In these games players must gather resources to construct buildings and build an army to defend against and defeat the opponent.

At the beginning of each game's match, it is important to gather as many resources as possible as fast as possible. It is a race to build defenses as quickly as you can. The only way to build an army is to collect enough resources to create them. You need soldiers, but you also need barracks and buildings to feed them. None of this is free. You need resources.

We need to harvest resources in our spiritual lives as well. We cannot expect to defend ourselves against temptation or grow in virtue without the necessary foundation. God provides for us the means to grow in our spiritual journeys. It is up to us to go out and find these ways to grow.

What kinds of resources enable us to grow in our spiritual life? Remember that for the Christian, the spiritual life is less about gathering skills and holy habits and more about growing in a relationship with God. Therefore, the question really becomes: What resources help us grow in a relationship with God?

Consider the following resources:

The Bible: Reading sacred Scripture helps us learn more about God and his people. God also speaks directly to us through the living Word. Sometimes when we read the Bible carefully, we will feel that God is speaking directly to us in a word or phrase that we read.

Prayer: Prayer is time spent with God. We pray by giving thanks and praise or asking for God's help for ourselves and for others. We can speak spontaneously in prayer or find pre-written prayers to help us find the right words to say to God in a certain time and place.

Sacraments: The sacraments of the Church continually provide the grace for us to grow in closer unity with Jesus Christ. Through the sacraments we become more like Christ as we are united more and more with him.

Gather these resources in your lives and grow in faith and your relationship with God.

CHAPTER 75
FARMING FOR FAITH

There is a tendency among Christians, especially amateur Christians, to think that spirituality should always be fun and inspired. One might think that being a Christian is all about great gifts of joy from God for being such good people. The fact is, however, living out our faith as Christians requires hard work and discipline.

The same goes for many video games, especially RPGs and MMORPGs, like *World of Warcraft*, that require you to gain experience points and items to level up. Gamers use the term "farming" or "grinding" to refer to the repetitive tasks that are often required to gain experience, items, or currency. Farming often means fighting the same monsters repeatedly to maximize the experience or hope that a magic item drops.

Farming for experience is tedious and boring. It is also essential for players that want to advance their characters enough to defeat the more difficult bosses. It may not be the most fun, but it makes advancing in the game much easier during the big battles and campaigns.

Jesus shared a few similar strategies with his disciples. In his Sermon on the Mount, he described three disciplines for Christians to practice quietly in secret: almsgiving, prayer, and fasting (Matthew 6:1–18). Just as grinding for experience is tedious and unrewarding in the short term, so too do these three disciplines seem unrewarding in the short term but beneficial for eternal life.

Jesus told the disciples to give alms (money to the poor) in secret and "your Father who sees in secret will reward you" (Matthew 6:4). He told them to pray in "your room and shut the door and pray to your Father who is in secret, and your Father who sees in secret will reward you" (Matthew 6:6). Finally, he told his disciples to give up food by fasting but not to appear hungry in front of others so that, once again, "your Father who sees in secret will reward you" (Matthew 6:18).

This requires a Christian to resist the temptation to appear righteous and holy for doing righteous things. Instead, to grow in holiness we must go farming as a part of our faith. We will grow in spiritual experience points so that we may stand up to the greatest temptations and overcome them to receive a much greater reward.

CHAPTER 76
MEGA MAN MASTERY

In Capcom's *Mega Man* (1987) a blue, humanlike robot sets out to defeat a collection of rogue robots with various abilities. These rogue robots, known as Robot Masters, possess unique and special powers that correlate to their names. The Robot Masters include Fire Man, Ice Man, Cut Man, Bomb Man, Wood Man, Bubble Man, Needle Man, Gemini Man, Snake Man, Drill Man, Pharaoh Man, Skull Man, and many more.

After defeating each of these Robot Masters at the end of their levels, Mega Man gains their abilities. He can then use those abilities to exploit a weakness and defeat another Robot Master. Players are given a choice for which robot level to attempt first and, therefore, which powers to use in future levels. For example, Fire Man is weak against Ice Man's abilities. Cut Man is weak against Guts Man's rock-like super arm. (Notice the inspiration from the classic rock-paper-scissors game?)

The Christian life can be much like Mega Man's mastery of new abilities. As Saint Paul wrote, "If anyone is in Christ, there is a new creation: everything old has passed away;

look, new things have come into being" (2 Corinthians 5:17). It is in Christ that we can overcome our greatest challenges. "I can do all things through him who strengthens me" (Philippians 4:13). In him we have new ability to defeat our inner enemies.

Every inner temptation or obstacle to grow and become a better person can be overcome in unique ways. We can try to defeat these inner enemies through hard work, but as Christians we find that turning to God for strength is a much better way. Just as Mega Man masters new abilities, God blesses us with the strength to overcome our greatest challenges.

CHAPTER 77
EVOLVE LIKE A POKÉMON

Trainers in the various *Pokémon* games help their pocket monsters gain experience and then evolve into stronger species of Pokémon. The happy little Charmander lizard, for example, evolves into Charmeleon, who can evolve into the great Charizard. Squirtle becomes Wartortle, who evolves into Blastoise.

Christians experience a similar transformation in their spiritual life. We call this conversion. Christians often speak about their "conversion moment," in which they meaningfully embraced their faith in God. In Greek the word is *metanoia*, which means literally "turning" and refers to someone changing their mind.

Like a Pokémon trainer leading a pocket monster to evolve, John the Baptist cried out in the desert, "Repent, and believe in the good news!" (Mark 1:15). Likewise, Jesus began his ministry proclaiming, "Repent, for the kingdom of heaven has come near" (Matthew 4:17).

To repent is to turn away from the old life and live a new one. Jesus later would say to his disciples, "If any wish to come after me, let them deny themselves and take up their cross daily and follow me" (Luke 9:23). We must die to our old selves and rise again anew, just as Jesus died and rose again. We must die to whatever bad habits or repetitive sins we committed in the past and turn toward God to live and love as he did.

In a similar way, Pokémon evolve into something new. Their old selves are gone and a new version exists in its place. The journey of a Christian, likewise, requires us to constantly evolve into someone spiritually new. We must die to our old selves and become someone new. The old version is gone and we evolve into a new version of ourselves with exciting new possibilities.

CHAPTER 18
HOW TO EVOLVE

In the core series of *Pokémon* games, evolution is possible in three ways:

1. Attain a certain level
2. Exposure to an item
3. Getting traded to another player

Let's look at Christian conversion in the same way. How are we to become new creations in Christ? How are we truly able to turn away from sin and repent so that we can live a new way of life?

Gain levels

In the spiritual life we level up by acquiring good habits called virtues. Saint Paul wrote about the highest of these virtues: faith, hope, and love. These virtues are gifts from God, and the more we grow in them, the closer we get to Jesus Christ. This leads to spiritual conversion that turns us into someone new. We become a different kind of person by the good habits we take up and practice daily.

Items

Many people can point to specific objects that led to their conversion experiences. Saint Augustine, for example, had his conversion moment reading a verse from the Bible. Similarly, many Christians can point to specific verses in the Bible that have been a source for transformation. Others can point to holy places or sacramental experiences of Jesus's presence that led to their conversion.

Trade

Some Pokémon can only evolve by being traded to another player. Likewise, many Christians experience their conversion moments through exposure to a new community. The great Christian writer C. S. Lewis, for example, came to faith largely through conversations with his fellow writing friends, including J. R. R. Tolkien.

It isn't always obvious how a Pokémon will evolve at first. It takes time and exploration of the game to reach a moment where they can be transformed. Similarly, a Christian conversion won't be obvious either, and the encounter with Christ will be different for everyone. God's plan eventually becomes known, and the calling to repent and change becomes unavoidable.

CHAPTER 79
CHEAT CODE

If you grew up playing Nintendo in the 1980s and '90s, then would you know exactly what this means:

UP, UP, DOWN, DOWN, LEFT, RIGHT, LEFT, RIGHT, B, A, SELECT, START

This, of course, is the legendary Konami Code, or Contra Code. The code can be used in many of the Konami company video games and non-Konami games that give a nod to the nostalgia of the most popular cheat code in the history of video games.

In the NES game *Contra*, entering the code right before selecting Start would add thirty extra lives for the player, making it much easier to get through the difficult game. The first issue of *Nintendo Power* (July/August 1988), which offered subscribers guides through many different game levels, featured the Contra Code. Nintendo gave away 3.6 million free copies of this first edition, and a love of cheat codes and Easter eggs was born.

So we have to ask: Is there a cheat code to get to heaven? Let's not call it cheating. Let's call it a shortcut or an easier path to holiness. It would have to be simple, like entering a code into a video game. Is there anything like this in the spiritual life?

A young Catholic nun in the nineteenth century thought so. Her name was Saint Therese of the Child Jesus, otherwise known as Saint Therese of Lisieux. She described a path of holiness she called the "Little Way."

She looked at the many amazing lives of her heroes, the saints, in comparison to her own simple spiritual life. She thought that if she wasn't going to become a famous, world-changing saint like Saint Francis of Assisi or Saint Teresa of Avila, then she could find a simpler path to holiness.

She thought of the Little Way like an elevator to heaven. Instead of trying to do great and holy deeds, she focused on small holy actions. The modern-day Mother Teresa, who took her name from Saint Therese, is often quoted as saying, "Not all of us can do great things, but we can do small things with great love."

The cheat code to get to heaven is simple. Instead of being a great and holy person, do small and holy things on a day-to-day basis. Clean the dishes. Pick up garbage. Give someone a compliment.

Most of all, put others before yourself. Jesus put it this way: "The last will be first, and the first will be last" (Matthew 20:16). The more you put others before yourself, the closer you will be to God, who became a servant to us all. Jesus "emptied himself, taking the form of a slave" and "humbled himself . . . to the point of death" (Philippians 2:7–8). The quickest path to heaven is exactly the same: humbly serve others.

CHAPTER 80
THE TOWER OF CRANKING 90S

In *Fortnite* players can build walls and structures to provide themselves a level of protection against the enemy. Some players use the phrase "cranking 90s" or "cranking" to describe a player who builds a tower quickly by turning 90 degrees repeatedly to build walls and ramps to gain height. Players can quickly create a tall tower and gain the advantage over their competitors with a strong defense and the high ground.

There were people in Genesis 11 with a similar idea. They built a tall tower up to the heavens for themselves, but this displeased God. As a punishment for trying to reach God on their own, the Lord scattered the people and divided them into groups speaking different languages. The place was called Babel because from that point forward, people began speaking other languages that sounded like babbling.

In *Fortnite* building a tower can be risky. Build it too high and you risk death by falling. A structure can leave you vulnerable because it stands out in the game's landscape. It's better not to let personal pride get in the way of making good decisions, like the people in Babel failed to do.

The message of the Babel story is echoed in a lesson Jesus taught many years later. He said that in order to be one of his disciples, they had to leave behind everything they had, including all possessions and even their families who loved them. It was a difficult message for the people to hear. Jesus compared the decision to follow him to building a tower: "For which of you, intending to build a tower, does not first sit down and estimate the cost, to see whether he has enough to complete it?" (Luke 14:28).

Are you willing to take the risk of discipleship? If so, you have to be humble. You cannot rely on family, friends, possessions, or anything other than God. Unlike the people of Babel, we must rely only on the Lord to build our towers. The more we give up, the more we are free to follow him.

CHAPTER 81
IGNORE THE DOG

In the mid-to-late 1980s the Nintendo Entertainment System was shipped with two games: *Super Mario Bros.* and *Duck Hunt*. The system came with the Nintendo Zapper, a gun that could be used in the *Duck Hunt* game. The goal of the game was exactly as it sounds—go duck hunting.

In *Duck Hunt* your trusty dog accompanies you during each level. The Duck Hunt Dog scares the ducks, and you are tasked with shooting them as quickly as possible. But if you miss all the ducks in a round, your dog stands up and laughs at you. It is hard not to get angry and annoyed with the dog as you advance through higher levels. He has been called the most disliked character in Nintendo history.

Jesus warned about this kind of character in the Christian life. In his Sermon on the Mount, he said: "Blessed are you when people revile you and persecute you and utter all kinds of evil against you falsely on my account. Rejoice and be glad, for your reward is great in heaven, for in the same way they persecuted the prophets who were before you" (Matthew 5:11–12).

Imagine rejoicing when the Duck Hunt Dog laughs at you. Instead of anger or self-loathing, you rejoice. It seems almost impossible.

But this joy is exactly what Jesus offers to his disciples. People don't find Christians funny—they find them ridiculous and out of touch. They see Christianity as wasting their time or believing in something childish. They see Christians failing to act like Christians and write off the entire religion because of those mistakes. They are like the Duck Hunt Dog laughing at a player who misses all the ducks.

Ignore the Duck Hunt Dog. Ignore the people who don't take Christianity seriously because of what they see. Being a Christian isn't easy. You will fail and leave yourself open for mockery and even evil words. Ignore them. Keep trying. Start another level and don't give up.

CHAPTER 82
GLHF YOUR ENEMIES

At the beginning of a match, gamers sometimes type "GLHF" to their opponents. GLHF stands for "good luck, have fun." The abbreviation had its origin in the 1990s multiplayer PC gaming world of *Quake*, *StarCraft*, and *Counter-Strike*. Players faced off and wished each other luck in the chat box before the games began. Players often ended matches with "GG" as well, meaning "good game."

Gamers could earnestly want another player to have fun and have good luck. They could say GLHF to wish an opponent or an ally luck. GLHF can certainly be used in the way Saint Paul recommended to the Thessalonians to "encourage one another and build up each other" (1 Thessalonians 5:11).

But GLHF can also be sent to an opponent with sarcasm. In other words, they might mean "good luck—you're going to need it!" From a Christian perspective, GLHF and GG are great practices when said in earnest, not sarcastically. Say it and mean it.

Jesus taught something shocking about how to relate to people who hate us. He said to "love your enemies; do good to those who hate you; bless those who curse you" (Luke 6:27–28). We don't have to like them. We don't have to want to spend time with them or hang out with them. But we do have to love our enemies and hope they do have good luck and have fun.

Love in this Christian sense does not mean affectionate feelings. It does not mean a physical or emotional attraction to another person. Jesus said to "love one another . . . as I have loved you" (John 13:34). This is a new commandment. How did he love us? He died for us. He gave up his life so that we could have life. In the same way, we should love even our enemies by hoping the best for them.

GLHF is a great gesture. We should always give our best against an opponent, but we shouldn't let competitiveness lead to hate. Instead, "love your enemies, do good, and lend, expecting nothing in return" (Luke 6:35). We may not receive GLHF back, but that's okay. The goal is to love our neighbor whether they love us back or not.

CHAPTER 83
CUTSCENES

Many video games, especially action-adventures and RPGs, maintain their story line through a series of cutscenes in between gameplay. Once players reach a certain point of the game, a movie-like scene begins with dialogue and action a player can only watch. Cutscenes existed as early as *Ninja Gaiden* in 1988. The scenes may maintain the same graphics as the main game, as with *Ninja Gaiden*, or shift to better-quality video. This was the case for *Final Fantasy VII*, in which the cutscenes shift from thirty-two bit to a full CGI-quality video with humanlike characters. The cutscenes in *Wing Commander IV* (1996) even featured an all-star cast in their cutscenes, with Mark Hamill (*Star Wars*), John Rhys-Davies (*Indiana Jones* and *The Lord of the Rings*), Malcolm McDowell (*Star Trek*), Tom Wilson (*Back to the Future*), and more.

Our lives are full of cutscenes. There are so many times in which we must relinquish control and let God's plan take place. In these moments it feels much like the scenes of a video game in which we set down the controller and watch the story line God is writing for us take place.

When the angel Gabriel appeared to the Virgin Mary, she chose to accept God's cutscene with a willing acceptance of his plan. "Here am I, the servant of the Lord," she said, "let it be with me according to your word" (Luke 1:38). Likewise, God has plans for us. He has a story in mind for us. Sometimes we need to follow Mary's example and let it be done to us. Accept the cutscenes and see the good plans God has in store for us.

What will we see? We don't know. We cannot plan for God's cutscenes in life. "What no eye has seen, nor ear heard, nor the human heart conceived, what God has prepared for those who love him" (1 Corinthians 2:9). But as Christians we remain ready to accept his will and carry out the story line. It may be difficult or it may be rewarding, like watching the beauty of a real-life cutscene in a game. "Open my eyes, so that I may behold wondrous things out of your law" (Psalm 119:18).

It can sometimes be easier to see the scenes in retrospect as memories. At the times we lost control, we had to rely on God. If we were courageous enough, we had to let go of our desire for control. If not, we suffered, like trying to take control of a player in the cutscenes. Look back and think about the moments God was at work in your life. Those moments might have been difficult at the time, but they are often filled with meaning for you today.

CHAPTER 84
THE JOYSTICK

Before the D-pad became the dominant video game controller style for home consoles, most video games were played with a joystick, especially in the arcade. Joysticks are often a short stick with a ball at the top to navigate the player character on the screen. The design took its original inspiration from the flight stick in an airplane. While the original Nintendo popularized the directional pad, the NES Advantage controller from the late 1980s gave gamers the arcade experience at home.

Navigating a game with a joystick is a good reminder for us. Joy is not a destination—it is a way of life. If we make joy or happiness a goal, then we are setting ourselves up for disappointment. Happiness is always fleeting. It comes and goes, but attaching happiness to a goal is dangerous. Applied to video games, it would be like thinking we can only be happy when we beat the game. No, it's the playing of the game that makes us happy. It's the playing that gives us joy, not reaching the end.

We rejoice today. We have joy by the way we live. "This is the day that the Lord has made; let us rejoice and be glad in it" (Psalm 118:24). Jesus gave his disciples a hint about this truth. He told his disciples to "abide in my love" and "keep my commandments" so that "my joy may be in you and that your joy may be complete" (John 15:9–11). Joy is not a reward. Joy is the byproduct of a way of life. When we live in the love of God and follow his commandments, we experience joy.

So many Christians seem to have a secret source of joy. They live differently. We love being around them. They are full of love and selflessness. They play the game of life with a joystick, not searching for joy as a reward for hard work but living joy right now in every moment. They play with a joystick way of life.

CHAPTER 85
DANCE DANCE DISCIPLES

Standard video game controllers only require the use of thumbs and sometimes index fingers. Some video games and video game systems enable a greater use of the body. The Wii Remote was a breakthrough that turned video gameplay into a full-body experience with its motion sensors. VR and AR video games require the greater use of the body as well. Even the original NES had the Power-glove and the Power Pad for running games. The Power Pad in the 1980s paved the way for one of the most successful games of the late 1990s and early 2000s, *Dance Dance Revolution*, which requires players to move their feet in imitation of the dance moves on the video game screen. The game is well-regarded for the physicality that is needed to win.

There is a tendency to think Christianity only focuses on spiritual things when, in fact, the body is essential to theology. God himself took on human form and had a body all his own. He died and rose again in his body. Likewise, we as Christians look forward to our own resurrection of the body at the second coming of Christ, when he will come to judge both the living and the dead, body and soul.

You cannot play *Dance Dance Revolution* without learning to move your body. Likewise, you cannot be a disciple without treating the body with respect. "Do you not know that your body is a temple of the Holy Spirit within you, which you have from God, and that you are not your own? . . . Therefore glorify God in your body" (1 Corinthians 6:19–20). Christians not only respect their own bodies, they intend to glorify God with their bodies "Whether you eat or drink or whatever you do, do everything for the glory of God" (1 Corinthains 10:31). Treat your body well, and remember that the Spirit of God lives within the body that God has given to you.

CHAPTER 86
SLACKING WITH SOLITAIRE

Solitaire is a classic solo card game that became a popular built-in video game for most computers in the last few decades. Playing *Solitaire* on a PC at work became a classic joke. People would take a break from boring work at their computer to play a few rounds of *Solitaire*. As a running joke, the game was commonly shown on computer screens in the background of scenes of the popular TV show *The Office*.

Work can be both difficult and boring, so we often avoid it. In fact, hard work is listed as one of the consequences of sin. "By the sweat of your face you shall eat bread until you return to the ground" (Genesis 3:19). So it is no wonder so many people avoid work to play challenging yet rewarding rounds of *Solitaire*.

We are called to persevere in our work. "Whatever task you must do, work as if your soul depends on it, as for the Lord and not for humans. . . . you serve the Lord Christ" (Colossians 3:23–24). *Solitaire* is an escape. It is a fun and meaningless accomplishment. Whether we work at a boring job, a thankless job, or our job is unending schoolwork, we must approach each task with determination. Remind yourself that we serve the Lord in all that we do. *Solitaire* is an escape from work but also an escape from the service of God. Yes, it is hard. It is supposed to be hard. Show up, do the work, and play *Solitaire* on your own time.

CHAPTER 87
SMASHING SPIRITUAL GIFTS

Super Smash Bros. is unlike other fighting games in one important way. Rather than trying to kill the opponent in a bloody battle, the fighters seek to score more points and eject a player out of bounds. To win, each of the classic Nintendo characters has unique attacks and abilities to remain on the screen. These abilities are wide-ranging and unique.

According to Saint Paul, each of us has unique spiritual gifts given to us by the Holy Spirit. "There are varieties of gifts but the same Spirit, and there are varieties of services but the same Lord, and there are varieties of activities, but it is the same God who activates all of them in everyone" (1 Corinthians 12:4–6). He goes on to describe gifts of wisdom, knowledge, faith, healing, powerful deeds, prophecy, discernment of spirits, speaking in tongues, and interpretation of tongues. He then describes the Church as a metaphor for Christ's body, with each of us serving in unique ways as unique parts of the body, such as hands or feet.

Ask yourself, what are your spiritual gifts? What are the ways in which the Holy Spirit has called you to serve the Lord? Donkey Kong's attacks in *Super Smash Bros.* are very different from those of Pikachu, Jigglypuff, or Mario. In the same way, you have strengths that make you stand out among others. God gives you these gifts not to kill, but to grow and improve. These are gifts not to compare yourself as better or worse, just different.

You will stand out among others and be recognized for these gifts. Like the last character standing in *Super Smash Bros.*, you will be complimented on your accomplishments. What are these successes? What are your gifts? Recognizing these abilities will help you think about the ways you can serve others and find happiness in the work you do. It will help you grow as an individual and grow in your ability to help carry out God's will in the world.

CHAPTER 88
SKILL TREES OF THE SPIRIT

In video game RPGs, players gain experience and increase their abilities and attributes in a variety of ways. *Diablo II* popularized a modern form of character building with visual representations of interconnected skills. Players gain experience and levels, then invest in specific attributes to increase the abilities they choose. The game *Civilization* (1991) first introduced the concept of a technology tree, which later inspired the skill trees in the *Diablo* series and other RPGs, like *Final Fantasy*, *Assassin's Creed*, *The Witcher*, and the *Elder Scrolls* series.

As Christians we also grow in certain abilities, but we call them gifts, not skills. These gifts are given by God the Holy Spirit. As Saint Paul said, "There are varieties of gifts but the same Spirit, and there are varieties of services but the same Lord, and there are varieties of activities, but it is the same God who activates all of them in everyone" (1 Corinthians 12:4–6). Unlike skill trees in video games, in which a player picks what skills to develop, our gifts are given and increased according to God's plan.

There are traditionally seven gifts of the Holy Spirit, inspired by the words of Isaiah 11:2–3: wisdom, understanding, counsel, fortitude, knowledge, piety, and fear of the Lord. God activates these gifts within us as we receive an outpouring of the Holy Spirit. The gifts are instilled in us in Christian baptism and strengthened through the anointing of confirmation.

If we think about the gifts of the Spirit like a spiritual gifts skill tree, then we can certainly turn to God and ask him to increase in us each of the gifts throughout our lives. "Pursue love and strive for spiritual gifts," writes Saint Paul (1 Corinthians 14:1). In prayer we can ask for the gifts we need the most in life at any point of our adventures. At times we will need to grow in the gifts of wisdom, understanding, knowledge, and counsel. At other times we will need fortitude to overcome fear. We may even need to humble ourselves with an increase in the gifts of piety and fear of the Lord.

But the important message to remember is that it is God, not us, who is working on our skill trees of the Spirit. He is the one working on a character build within us. A part of being a Christian is discerning which gifts God has given to us. Then we can embrace our gifts and the character class God desires for us. Otherwise, if we choose to ignore our gifts, we will struggle to be who we are meant to become. We will be happier and more at peace if we welcome God's gifts and apply them in our lives as we grow and overcome our greatest challenges.

PART SIX
BEATING THE GAME

CHAPTER 89
ENDLESS RUNNERS

While most classic video games have levels with a beginning and an end, the genre of endless runners (or infinite runners) includes a never-ending level to explore. Endless runners were especially popular as mobile games, including *Jetpack Joyride*, *Subway Surfers*, and the game that popularized the format, *Temple Run*. Nintendo's first mobile game, *Super Mario Run*, was actually an endless runner.

It is hard to grasp the concept of infinity. In an endless runner, players collect coins and avoid obstacles to get a high score before failing. The game goes on forever regardless of when the player dies. The similarities to the spiritual life should be obvious.

As Christians we believe in the concept of infinity. God has no beginning and no end. This includes all three persons of the Trinity: Father, Son, and Holy Spirit. The Bible begins with this important truth, explaining, "In the beginning, when God created . . ." (Genesis 1:1). The Holy Spirit was there, too, as the "spirit" or "wind from God [that] swept over the face of the waters" (Genesis 1:2). The

Gospel of John attests to Christ's presence as well in its opening line: "In the beginning was the Word, and the Word was with God, and the Word was God" (John 1:1).

God has no beginning and no end. "Jesus Christ is the same yesterday and today and forever" (Hebrews 13:8). As Jesus proclaimed in Revelation, "I am the Alpha and the Omega, the First and the Last, the Beginning and the End" (Revelation 22:13). *Alpha* and *Omega* are the first and last letters of the Greek alphabet. God has always been and always will be.

We, however, have a beginning like the endless-runner video games. We will also have an end, even if the level continues to go on infinitely. Yet we run with a purpose. "Surrounded by so great a cloud of witnesses, let us also lay aside every weight and the sin that clings so closely, and let us run with perseverance the race that is set before us, looking to Jesus" (Hebrews 12:1–2). What awaits us at the end of the race? "You will win the crown of glory that never fades away" (1 Peter 5:4). Free from sin and following in the footsteps of Christ, we will live on endlessly even after our deaths. Just as Jesus Christ has no end—so too will our lives go on infinitely as we remain close to him.

CHAPTER 90
ALTERNATE ENDINGS

Early video games, like books and films before them, had a singular ending. As storytelling in games advanced, however, and more choices were added during gameplay, it became possible for game developers to include multiple endings. In these "choices matter" games, the endings will change either drastically or slightly based on conversations during the game, unlocked items, or how much of the story you uncovered while you played.

The classic SNES version of *Chrono Trigger*, for example, had at least twelve endings. *Resident Evil* included four endings for each character in the original video game. *Fallout 3* has four endings with variants, and the *Mass Effect* series includes two to three endings in each game.

Choices matter in life too. The choices we make either lead us closer to God or further away from him. As you know, the choices that hurt our relationship with God and others are called sins. When we accept the grace and mercy of God, we grow closer in his love with him and his people.

Which brings us to the multiple endings in store for us. After we die each of us will be judged by God. Our souls will either be destined for heaven or sent into eternal separation from God. Why? Because choices matter. The way we play the game of life will lead us into multiple endings.

When Christ comes to judge the living and the dead, he explained that those who denied him "will go away into eternal punishment but the righteous into eternal life" (Matthew 25:46). Jesus described this eternal punishment as "the eternal fire prepared for the devil and his angels" (Matthew 25:41). We don't like to think or talk about this much, but hell is real. Our choices matter, and if we choose to turn away from God and his people, then we will remain apart from him.

Thankfully, we should not lose hope. God loves all his people, and those who accept his love and love him back are on the way to a happy heavenly ending. "What no eye has seen, nor ear heard, nor the human heart conceived, what God has prepared for those who love him" (1 Corinthians 2:9). Jesus Christ suffered, died, and rose again so that we could always come back to the Lord and rise with him.

Your endings are not rewards and punishments for how well you played the game. The endings are based on whether you loved God or not. Choose to love God and his people in life, and you will remain in his love forever. It is not always easy. Choose to turn away from God's love or choose to selfishly deny love of others, and your end will be to remain apart from him. It's a natural consequence for the end of life to match the way the game of life was played.

CHAPTER 91
HIGH SCORE

Getting your name or initials on the high-score board of your favorite game was a badge of honor in the arcade video game. When a game wasn't being played in an arcade, the screen would show a leaderboard with the best scores. Most of the time the board only had room for initials, so players got creative (and sometimes irreverent) in displaying their three-letter names.

It was great to have bragging rights in front of your friends. It promoted more playing as well. Any time your score was beat, you felt the motivation to play more and get your score to show up again on the leaderboard. Extra visits to the arcade or restaurant with the game led to more attempts and a lot more quarters. Defending your title seemed to be an endless task.

This was the main problem with displaying high scores on the arcade games. The success never lasted. Either your initials were defeated by a higher score, or an error in the game required the owners to unplug or reboot the game, erasing all of the high scores.

The high-score mentality is something we see in every part of life. People are motivated not just by personal success but by being better than others. Competition helps, but the feeling of superiority can become a real driver for people.

The sad part of the pursuit of success is that it never lasts. Like trying to keep your initials on the screen of high scores, success in either fame or financial wealth falls away. "Do not love the world or the things in the world. . . . And the world and its desire are passing away, but those who do the will of God abide forever" (1 John 2:15, 17). Remember, God isn't keeping score. It does not matter how much better you are at the game of life than others.

High scores pass away. Wealth passes away. Social media followers, job titles, salaries, fancy cars, and big houses are all fleeting. After all those things are gone, all that remains is our closeness to God and our neighbors.

CHAPTER 92

GOD DOESN'T KEEP SCORE

Many video games keep track of how many points a player scores as they play. The better you perform, the higher your score. In some games scoring as many points as possible is the main goal of the game.

It's possible that a scoreboard is the biggest misconception about God. God doesn't keep score. His judgment is not based on a scoreboard in the sky. We so often mistakenly think God is adding or subtracting points to our spiritual scoreboard as we go through life. A sin does not subtract points of a score. God doesn't have a scoreboard.

When Jesus described the Last Judgment in Matthew 25, he used a metaphor of separating sheep from goats. The sheep were the ones who fed the hungry, welcomed strangers, and served the sick, poor, and imprisoned. The goats were the ones that didn't help others. No one received bonus points for the number of people they helped. When they helped anyone in need, they were helping Jesus. The goal is to grow closer to Jesus, not score points to impress a sacred scorekeeper.

In the original *Super Mario Bros.*, Mario and Luigi score points for defeating enemies, collecting items and coins, and breaking bricks. To win the game, however, you only have to save the princess. The points are, in fact, pointless. The score has no impact on winning the game. The only thing that matters is progress toward the princess.

The same goes for the Christian life. God will not judge you based on how many spiritual points you scored in life. Judgment is based upon progress, not points. Love God and love your neighbor. Love and running toward the Lord are what matter most.

God is not waiting for us to succeed or fail. He is intimately involved in our lives right now. He sends help so we won't fail. He even sent his only Son to sacrifice himself and sent the Holy Spirit so we would not be alone. Any failure isn't final. There is no final score. God's mercy is endless and offered continually as we play the game of life.

CHAPTER 93
CROSSING INTO PARADISE

The *Animal Crossing* series of Nintendo games offers countless hours of fun for creative gamers. The games are open-ended without specific levels or goals, giving players the freedom to create a world just the way they like it. Whether designing an island resort on the Nintendo Switch or a campsite on a mobile version of *Animal Crossing*, players will explore, create, and connect with other players and animals.

The world is a happy place in the game. There are no dark enemies or evil bosses to defeat. Players create a paradise and have fun making friends along the way.

As Christians we work with the Lord to create a spiritual paradise and make friends along the way as well. In the terminology of his time, Jesus described this paradise as the kingdom of heaven (or kingdom of God). John the Baptist joined Jesus and the apostles in proclaiming a key message to all who would hear it: "Repent, for the kingdom of heaven has come near" (Matthew 3:2).

Jesus also described the kingdom as a house much like the tents, houses, and resorts players build in *Animal Crossing*. Heaven is a house that welcomes all, just like the animals are welcome in the game. "In my Father's house there are many dwelling places," he said. "If it were not so, would I have told you that I go to prepare a place for you?" (John 14:2).

What a comfort to know that Jesus Christ has created a paradise for us in the kingdom of heaven. He welcomes us not as servants but as his friends (John 15:15). Likewise, we work with him to create some semblance of the kingdom here on earth and welcome people into the Church. Together we will find joy in everyday life and look forward to the day we will join Jesus in the paradise of his happy home.

CHAPTER 94
BURY YOUR BADGES

Many video games include badges and trophies as an extra level of motivation to keep playing the game. Completing tasks, challenges, and mini-quests within a game can unlock achievements that will appear in a virtual showcase in the game. Online networks for games on the PlayStation, Xbox, Apple Game Center and more offer different versions of achievements to show off to friends. Habit tracking apps and educational platforms often use badges and achievements to add a level of gamification as well.

Players can feel pride in their achievements. It is hard to resist the desire to pursue an in-game challenge to unlock an achievement. Players will invest a lot of time and effort into earning a badge and bolstering their showcase. After many years, they will build up large collections of badges and trophies.

Even in Jesus's time, trophies were given as rewards in games. Saint Paul used prizes for runners in a race as a metaphor to express the goal of the Christian life. "Run in such a way that you may win it. Athletes exercise self-control in all things; they do it to receive a perishable wreath, but we an imperishable one" (1 Corinthians 9:24–25). It is no coincidence that many video game achievements and trophies are designed with wreaths as an outline. Wreaths were the trophies in the ancient world and worn as crowns. Even today, track medalists often wear wreaths after they win.

The key point that Saint Paul made when talking about trophies and competition is to look at life like a race. The only crown that matters is the imperishable one—the "crown of righteousness" (2 Timothy 4:8). All other trophies, achievements, and badges will fall away.

The message is similar to Jesus's Parable of the Rich Fool (Luke 12:13–21). A rich man owned a farm that produced so much food he didn't know what to do with it. So, he tore down his barns and built larger ones to store all the extra grain. He dreamed of the celebration he would have after all his achievements were safely stored in the new barns. But that very night the rich man died and he didn't get to take any of the goods with him.

What are your crowning achievements in life? What badges are you most proud of at home, school, and work? Be prepared to bury them. You can't take them with you when you die. Instead, always focus on unlocking the ultimate achievement, the imperishable badge of righteousness. Keep faith and put God as the goal above all other challenges you take on in life. All that matters is how close you are to him. He will give you a reward that lasts forever.

CHAPTER 95
VIDEO GAME MUSIC

What would a presentation of video games be without mention of the incredible music? Decades after playing video games in their youth, players still sing the familiar background music of their favorite games. Ask anyone growing up in the 1980s to sing the tunes of the eight-bit era games like *Super Mario Bros.* and *The Legend of Zelda*. The musical themes remain a vital part of the gaming experience. Classic JRPGs (Japanese role-playing games) like *Final Fantasy* and *Chrono Trigger* are well known for the impact of their musical scores despite the sound-chip limitations. Today epic symphonies are used to compose the music to match the level of special effects.

In many ways music plays an important background role in salvation history as well. Psalms is an entire book of the Bible dedicated to providing lyrics to lost melodies of thanks and praise to God. These psalms, as well as early Christian hymns, are featured in the New Testament as well, though their tunes are also lost in history.

One thing is certain—there is a constant reminder to turn to music to sing praise and thanks to God. "The Lord is my strength and my shield; in him my heart trusts; so I am helped, and my heart exults, and with my song I give thanks to him" (Psalm 28:7). "I will be glad and exult in you; I will sing praise to your name, O Most High" (Psalm 9:2). How can we keep from singing? As Saint James put it, "Are any [of you] cheerful? They should sing songs of praise" (James 5:13).

As we sing songs of praise, thanksgiving, and even lamentation here on earth, we look forward to the day we will join the chorus of heaven. When Jesus was born, the shepherds in the fields saw the angels praising God with "Glory to God in the highest heaven, and on earth peace among those whom he favors!" (Luke 2:14). We will one day join with these angels as saints in heaven, singing a new song, "worthy is the Lamb," who is Jesus Christ (Revelation 5:12).

Video game music plays on in the background repeatedly and without stopping. Music surrounds us. It is a part of our lives, and it will again be a part of eternal life in heaven. We will be united as one with God and the saints, singing an unending song of praise and thanks to God for our salvation. Not only will we sing a tune catchier than the beeps of the original Nintendo, we will not be able to contain ourselves and the joy welling up inside our souls.

CHAPTER 96
WE ARE THE PRINCESS

In the early popular Nintendo games like *Super Mario Bros.* and *The Legend of Zelda*, the goal is to save the princess. Saving a damsel in distress is a popular trope in fairy tales, books, and movies. This common goal made it an easy purpose for early video games as well.

We like to think of ourselves as the heroes of our own stories. You are, in fact, the hero in most of the gospel metaphors in this book. The truth is, however, we are not the heroes of our story. We think the game of life is about us.

If we gave our game a title, it would probably include our own names. While the title of the game of our lives may include our names, we are not the heroes. We are like Princess Zelda in the video game titled *The Legend of Zelda*. Link, not Zelda, is the hero. Link saves Princess Zelda.

Who is our hero? Who is constantly at work to save us? Who gives up their life for us? Jesus Christ, of course, is the hero of our story.

Often throughout the Bible, God's people are described as a bride. The Church is the Bride of Christ (Ephesians 5:22–23). We are like the princess, and Christ is like the hero who saves us. He is the reason for our salvation. We do not and cannot save ourselves. We are trapped, and we need him to come for us.

The good news is he is already here. He has already completed the quest. We are in the end screen and the hero has saved us. Do you know what Princess Zelda and Princess Peach say to their heroes at the end of the games? "Thank you." May we all have the humility to say the same to our hero, Jesus Christ.

CHAPTER 97
THE SECOND QUEST

After saving the princess from the clutches of Bowser in the last level of the original Nintendo's *Super Mario Bros.*, we are rewarded with the following message: "Thank you, Mario! Your quest is over. We present you a new quest. Push Button B to select a world."

Likewise, after defeating Gannon and freeing Princess Zelda in *The Legend of Zelda*, she says: "Thanks, Link, you're the hero of Hyrule. Finally peace returns to Hyrule. This ends the story."

But after the credits, we read: "Another quest will start from here. Press the Start button."

Each game offers a second quest. The great victory is followed by another adventure. In *Super Mario Bros.*, the platforms are smaller and the monsters are tougher to defeat. Likewise, *The Legend of Zelda*'s second quest is more difficult, with changes to the dungeon locations and maps.

Eternal life is like our second quest. It will be a new and exciting adventure. What will this second quest be like? We don't know for sure. As Saint John wrote, "What we will be has not yet been revealed. What we do know is this: when he is revealed, we will be like him, for we will see him as he is" (1 John 3:2).

Think about heaven as the new and greatest adventure. It will not be some passive existence of heavenly boredom but a new quest about which we cannot comprehend. It will be the new and greatest adventure for all of us.

CHAPTER 98
END GAME CREDITS

Most video games end a lot like movies. You beat the game, watch a scene or two of an epilogue, then the post-credits roll down the screen. You see the name of everyone who worked on the game, including producers, directors, designers, programmers, composers, voice actors, and more.

The Christian life is a lot like this too. At the end of our lives, we can certainly be happy for our efforts. As Saint Paul wrote, "I have fought the good fight; I have finished the race; I have kept the faith" (2 Timothy 4:7). But we were never alone. Always, there were people there to help and support us along the way. Remember the words of the old man at the beginning of *The Legend of Zelda*? "You don't have to go alone." We didn't. We had help all along the way.

At the end of your life, think of all the people that you will need to give credit to for finishing the race. Think of the family and friends who were and will be there for you through life. Think of the many people you do not know in the Church and in heaven who supported you through prayer. You are never alone, and you will always have a list of people to thank as you finish the video game of life.

CHAPTER 99
LEVEL 99

Level 99 is the highest level we can achieve in many RPG video games. In early eight-bit games, this might have been limited by memory space to keep levels at a single byte of data. But even in later RPGs like *Final Fantasy, Chrono Trigger, Secret of Mana, Dragon Quest, Fallout 2* and *4*, stats and levels are often capped at 99 to keep character abilities at a reasonable level. Sports games like *John Madden Football* also cap skills at 99 to keep player abilities at a reasonable level. Designers had to set the maximum level somewhere, and 99 became a classic number to use as the cap.

At a certain point, we may reach this level in our own journey toward God. Saint Paul felt this way about his journey as a disciple. He had achieved level 99. He "fought the good fight" (2 Timothy 4:7). He was ready for "the crown of righteousness, which the Lord, the righteous judge" would give him on the day of judgment, along with all who longed for Jesus's return (2 Timothy 4:8).

At any time in our lives, we can pause and reflect on our experience of faith. Have we made progress in our spiritual skills that lead us closer to Christ? There is no way for sure to know when we will feel we have reached level 99. We don't have access to a dashboard with all our life stats. We do, however, know where our heart lies. Is it with the Lord? Is he still our one, true goal in the game of life? If so, we can be sure that level 99 is on the horizon. We can be sure that beating the game and being with God is our destiny.

NOTES

AUTHOR'S NOTE

1. C. S. Lewis, *Mere Christianity* (New York City, NY: HarperCollins Publishers, 2001), viii.

11. HYRULE OF HEAVEN

1. Andrew Vestal, "The History of Zelda," *GameSpot*, September 14, 2000.

19. GOD OR DEMIGOD?

1. United States Conference of Catholic Bishops, www.usccb.org/prayers/nicene-creed.
2. Saint Athanasius, *De incarnatione*, 54, 3.

70. PUSH PAUSE

1. *The Book of Her Life*, 8,5 in *The Collected Works of St. Teresa of Avila*, tr. K. Kavanaugh, OCD, and O. Rodriguez, OCD (Washington DC: Institute of Carmelite Studies, 1976)

In this early 1990s photograph Jared Dees is playing Super Nintendo and carefully studying a copy of *Nintendo Power* magazine.

ABOUT THE AUTHOR

JARED DEES is the creator of The Religion Teacher (TheReligionTeacher.com), a popular website that provides practical resources and teaching strategies for religious educators. A respected graduate of the Alliance for Catholic Education (ACE) program at the University of Notre Dame, Dees holds master's degrees in education and theology, both from Notre Dame. He frequently gives keynotes and leads workshops at conferences, church events, and school in-services throughout the year on a variety of topics. He lives near South Bend, Indiana, with his wife and children.

Learn more about Jared's books, speaking events, and other projects at jareddees.com.

ALSO BY JARED DEES

Made in United States
North Haven, CT
23 April 2024

51669676R00128